Behaviour Problems in the Early Years

What can be done to identify and manage behaviour problems in the early years?

This book addresses the issue of behaviour problems in the early years, offering early years practitioners a practical and well-researched resource, covering subjects such as:

- the nature and extent of behaviour problems in the early years;
- definitions and factors associated with behaviour problems;
- theoretical frameworks for screening, assessment and management;
- a blueprint for early identification and intervention.

The author shows that successful early identification and management of behaviour problems requires informed practice that takes into account existing theoretical and conceptual frameworks and makes systematic use of evidence. All professionals working in an early years environment will find this an invaluable read.

Theodora Papatheodorou is Reader in Early Childhood at the School of Education, Anglia Polytechnic University.

Behaviour Problems in the Early Years

A guide for understanding and support

Theodora Papatheodorou

RoutledgeFalmer
Taylor & Francis Group

LONDON AND NEW YORK

First published 2005
by RoutledgeFalmer
2 Park Square, Milton Park, Abingdon, Oxon OX14 4RN

Simultaneously published in the USA and Canada
by RoutledgeFalmer
270 Madison Ave, New York, NY 10016

RoutledgeFalmer is an imprint of the Taylor & Francis Group

© 2005 Theodora Papatheodorou

Typeset in Palatino and Gill by BC Typesetting Ltd, Bristol
Printed and bound in Great Britain by
TJ International Ltd, Padstow, Cornwall

British Library Cataloguing in Publication Data
A catalogue record for this book is available from the British Library

Library of Congress Cataloging in Publication Data
A catalog record for this book has been requested

ISBN 0–415–28697–2 (hbk)
ISBN 0–415–28698–0 (pbk)

This book is dedicated
to

Dimitri, my son,
with thanks for having taught me
so much with his thoughtfulness and maturity,

Janet, Arlene, Carl
Eleni and Spyro,
for their discreet support and for honouring me
with a lifelong friendship,

All my pupils,
especially those whom I may not always have served
as I should, with my deepest apologies.

All behaviour serves a purpose

Contents

Figures

Forms

Tables

Tables

Preface

Background information

As a nursery teacher, I worked with young children for almost fifteen years and, looking back, I can barely remember any children exhibiting behaviour problems. It was the same for my colleagues when, in the late 1980s and early 1990s, I conducted research into young children's behaviour problems and the management techniques used (Papatheodorou 1990, 1993). In the light of a child-centred philosophy influenced by developmental psychology, young children's behaviours were interpreted and referred to as developmental milestones which are expected to pass with time rather than difficulties which may have long-lasting effects.

However, nursery teachers' replies to my research provided a wide range of statements describing behaviours which were perceived as being problematic in the particular context of the nursery class. Despite the overall resistance to talking about behaviour problems among young children, the nursery teachers described a range of behaviours, including aggressive and withdrawn behaviours as well as language and communication difficulties and lack of motor skills, which were identified as being problematic in the particular context of the nursery class. The findings indicated that, although a number of young children's behaviours were 'developmentally related' (such as communication difficulties and lack of motor skills), these behaviours did raise just as much concern as acting out and excessively withdrawn behaviours, because of the demands and characteristics of the particular context of the nursery class, indicating that behaviour is not 'context free'.

With regard to behaviour management, the nursery teachers reported the use of a wide range of techniques of different

theoretical orientations. However, it was less clear whether their
decisions were guided by any specific theoretical orientation or
were just a 'pick and mix' of strategies which were perceived as
'working' with young children. Again, although these techniques
were reported as being good and effective practice for managing
behaviour in general, when employed with individual children
their effectiveness was less clear. More recently, some insightful
observations with regard to behaviour management and, especially,
the implementation of behaviour intervention plans have been
made by nursery teachers who have worked on a range of real-
life case studies, as part of their continuing professional development. The nursery teachers showed awareness of the importance
of planning for intervention that aims to meet the needs of individual children; however, they were less clear about the need to
(i) identify the criteria to be used and (ii) develop a monitoring
system, in order to demonstrate the successful implementation
and effectiveness of interventions (Papatheodorou 2002a). These
observations supported the view that emphasis should now be
placed on training that informs evidence-based practice in order
to meet the needs of individual children rather than on acquiring
skills for the implementation of packages and programmes
accepted for their effectiveness (Visser 2002; Barrett 2000).

The purpose of the book

This book aims to provide an overview of the field of behaviour
problems on the basis of extensive research undertaken in the
UK, the USA and other countries, and the author's own research
and subsequent work in the field. More importantly, the book
intends to provide a framework for early identification of, intervention for, and prevention of behaviour problems. The proposed
framework is informed by, and builds upon the principles of, early
years practice which aims to support children's holistic development by considering their particular ecosystems.

The book is based on the belief that concerns expressed about
and for children's behaviour should be substantiated by evidence
and interpreted in the light of sound relevant theories and knowledge. Systematic recording and monitoring of evidence and its
critical evaluation are important processes that should underline
practice claiming to meet the needs of individual children.
Ultimately, the book is intended to promote 'understanding,' pro-

viding a blueprint for good practice rather than offering a range of 'ready-made' strategies or panaceas for replication.

Structure of the book

The book consists of two parts. Part One includes five chapters which aim to provide a basis for understanding the nature of behaviour problems in the early years. Chapter One discusses the increased concerns about the rising incidence of behaviour problems among young children, acknowledging the debates surrounding issues such as the nature of behaviour problems in this particular age group and the difficulties surrounding their identification. Six real studies are outlined to illustrate the wide range of behaviours that may be of concern in early years settings.

Chapter Two looks, in detail, at the nature, extent and seriousness of behaviour problems among young children in the light of relevant research. Age and gender, being identified as particular variables associated with specific behaviours, are discussed and the debate about the continuity and discontinuity of problem behaviours, as children grow older, is addressed. The lack of agreed definitions, methodological issues, and the particular attitudes of those who judge children's behaviours as problematic are also discussed as important factors that affect the prevalence and nature of the reported behaviour problems.

Chapter Three is devoted to the conceptualisation of behaviour problems in general, that is, the terminology and definitions used in the field. Different terms and definitions, past and present, used mainly in policy documents and by administrative bodies, are discussed to illustrate that there is no single definition that satisfies professionals who come from different disciplines or have different background knowledge, training and responsibilities. It is argued, in this chapter, that professionals who work together should explicitly acknowledge the terminology and definitions which they use, and agree on shared definitions which ensure a use of language that minimises potential damage to children and has operational and functional value.

Chapter Four examines what constitutes problem behaviour within educational and early years settings to show that educators are guided not by any particular theoretical model regarding the definition of behaviour problems but by the pragmatics of the particular educational context. Problem behaviours in educational settings are seen as 'out of place' behaviours and are understood as being in a continuum which ranges from extremely difficult and/or problematic (either acting out/aggressive or withdrawn) to appropriate or desirable behaviour. Different systems of classifying behaviour problems are also discussed in this chapter to offer educators the knowledge and common ground needed to work with professionals from other disciplines. This chapter also sets out a cognitive-affective framework for understanding young children's behaviour, well-being and problem behaviours.

Chapter Five is devoted to factors associated with or considered to be influential sources of and influences on children's problem behaviours. These factors are examined at three levels of functioning to illustrate the contextual nature of behaviour problems, that is:

i.   the micro-level (e.g. the family, the early years setting/school and the child her/himself);
ii. the meso-level which represents the dynamic interrelationships within and between the different systems. As problem behaviours in educational settings are increasingly being understood in relation to the interactions of the persons involved, particular emphasis is placed on the interaction process between children and educators;
iii. the macro-level which represents policies and societal attitudes and values.

Part Two of the book consists of six chapters that refer to early identification and management of behaviour problems. Chapter Six briefly refers to a range of habitual behaviour management techniques which aim to create environments that facilitate appropriate behaviour and, ultimately, prevent the occurrence of problem behaviours. Chapter Seven discusses different approaches to behaviour management in the light of the different theoretical approaches that have influenced, and still influence, the field of education. Counselling and expressive arts and play are discussed in the light of the psychoeducational approach, and behaviour change is outlined in the light of underlying principles of the behavioural approach. Social skills training and emotional literacy are discussed as part of the cognitive-affective model, concluding with an ecosystemic approach which emphasises the important role of an empathetic understanding of children's behaviour problems and advocates a whole school/early years setting approach to promote positive behaviour support.

Chapter Eight deals with the screening process used to detect as early as possible potential difficulties which may be experienced by young children. Issues surrounding the screening and its potential pitfalls and limitations are discussed as well as the potential of the screening process for developing preventative structures and practices. A model for screening is suggested and emotional literacy is discussed as a means of supporting emotional and social competencies in young children. Particular emphasis is placed on storytelling and playing.

Chapter Nine is devoted to the assessment process which, in some cases, may need to follow initial screening to assess systematically the needs of individual children whose behaviour either raises serious concerns or is ambiguous and unclear. An integrated model for play-based and multi-purpose assessment is proposed in order to assess the functions of the behaviour within its particular context(s). The chapter offers a blueprint for the collection of information from multiple sources (parents, children, practitioners and other professionals) and for multiple purposes (identify specific behaviours and their functions and inform intervention) through play-based activities to devise an intervention action plan which, consequently, informs the development of a behaviour intervention plan.

Planning for intervention at different levels of functioning is the focus of Chapter Ten. Behaviour intervention plans are discussed as well as their monitoring and evaluation in order to determine the success, or otherwise, of their implementation and effectiveness. Chapter Eleven is devoted to both personal and professional traits, knowledge, skills and competencies required by early years practitioners/teachers to deal effectively with young children's problem behaviours. These include self-awareness and the ability to identify one's own strengths and limitations as well as the ability to establish collaborative ethos and partnership with other colleagues, parents and other professionals, services and agencies. This discussion impinges on the issue of continuing professional development which must be seen as a learning processes that emphasises evidence-based practice that is supported by sound conceptual frameworks rather than the teaching of specific programmes and strategies for replication.

Main features of the book

Each chapter of the book ends with a section entitled 'Concluding remarks' to summarise the key points/issues discussed, providing quick reference for busy practitioners. This section is followed by suggested short activities to be undertaken in order to allow early years practitioners and teachers to relate the issues discussed to their own practice. In several chapters, a number of tools (listed as 'forms') have been suggested for screening, assessment and intervention. These tools are only indicative and early years practitioners and teachers are expected to exercise their professional judgement in using them depending on the demands of particular cases.

Terminology used

Usually the term *behaviour problems* is used, mainly by psychologists, to indicate acting out and externalised behaviours that have a disturbing effect on others and the environment. In this book the term behaviour problems is used as an umbrella term to indicate a range of social, emotional and behavioural difficulties which, independently of their origins and functions, interfere with the child's own and others' well-being and learning. The term *problem behaviour* will be used to refer to the problematic nature of specific behaviours rather than the child's overall behaviour profile. Other terms will be used as they appear in the relevant literature.

The term early years refers to the life span between 0 and 8 years old. In this book, the terms *early years* and *young child* will refer mainly to children from three to six years old who attend some kind of early years statutory and/or non-statutory provision. It is appreciated that in some countries five- and six-year-olds may attend compulsory education (e.g. infant or primary schools), whereas in other countries they may attend preschools. The term *early years setting/class* will be used to reflect the diversity of provision offered for young children in a variety of settings in the maintained, voluntary and private sectors. The terms *early years practitioner/teacher* will be used to refer to a wide range of practitioners and professionals who, in different roles, are responsible for the education and care of young children for long periods of time and for a considerable part of the day. It is important to note that the use of these terms by no means assumes the same responsibilities or level of training and competencies for all those who work with children. The terms *educational setting* and *educators* will also be used, respectively, to refer to general education settings and all the professionals involved in the education of children. Other terms will be used as they appear in the literature. The personal pronouns *s/he, her/him* and *hers/his* will be used to refer to female and male gender.

Clarifications and disclaimer

The book is written on the assumption that early years practitioners/teachers have a good and critical understanding of young children's holistic development, and the knowledge and skills to implement early years curricula through play by considering the particular aspects of children's immediate and broader ecosystems. The tools suggested in this book are only indicative and they are not the only ones, nor necessarily the best. Early years practitioners and teachers have a professional responsibility to keep informed and updated about developments in the field so that they can make informed decisions and judgements about the choice of instruments, as well as how many of them they need to use depending on the complexity and severity of individual cases.

Finally, I must acknowledge my struggle and, sometimes, frustration in writing this book, as I may not have always communicated my understanding, knowledge and beliefs about the complexities of, and dynamic influences on, children's inner worlds and explicit behaviours, nor the demands which they make upon professional practice. According to Jacoby (1999: 53), 'Only part of the original, global experience can be expressed in words. The rest remains inaccurately named and poorly understood.' This assertion is especially true for the 'written word'.

Acknowledgements

I would like to thank my colleague and friend Janet Gill for her wholehearted support during the writing of this book. She read it repeatedly and thoroughly and provided constructive comments on the initial and final drafts of all chapters, always maintaining high interest, and kept me going when I despaired and thought that it would never be completed, as teaching, tutorials and other commitments overwhelmed me and the writing of the book became the least of my priorities. However, I am wholly responsible for any limitations in the book, as I have not always taken on board all constructive criticisms and comments. Thank you, Janet. I would also like to express my gratitude to Arlene Thomas-Ramasut who sensitively and constructively guided me during my initial research into behaviour problems. She has been a great mentor to me and a good friend for life. Thank you, Arlene.

Thanks are due to all nursery teachers, whose work on a number of case studies provided me with insightful observations and comments regarding the management of behaviour problems. I also thank Routledge for the kind permission to reproduce in this book the 'Checklist for pragmatic skills' from the book Wilson, R. *Special Educational Needs in the Early Years* (1998: 96–97). My sincere thanks also go to Professor Stephen Weiss for allowing me to quote his views regarding the psychoeducational approach, expressed in personal communication. My sincere appreciation also goes to Alison Foyle, the commissioning editor, who has waited patiently for the finished manuscript of this book.

Finally, I am totally indebted to my son, Dimitri, for his encouragement and support during the writing of this book and all my previous endeavours. Thank you, son, and I promise that you can now have the computer back and my devoted attention, until my next project.

Theodora Papatheodorou, 2004

Abbreviations

APA	American Psychiatric Association
BPCL	Problem Behaviour Checklist
DES	Department of Education and Science
DfE	Department for Education
DfEE	Department for Education and Employment
DfES	Department for Education and Skills
DoH	Department of Health
DSM	Diagnostic Statistical Manual
EYs	Early Years
GAP	Group for the Advancement of Psychiatry
HO	Home Office
IDEA	Individuals with Disabilities Education Act
IEP	Individual Educational Plan
LSA	Learning Support Assistant
NPPS	National Programme for Playground Safety
QCA	Qualifications and Curriculum Authority
RNIB	Royal National Institute for the Blind
SENCO	Special Educational Needs Coordinator
TES	*Times Educational Supplement*

Part I

Understanding behaviour problems

Chapter 1

Behaviour problems in the early years

An issue for concern?

The importance placed on academic achievement clearly underpins current policy and the research agenda that is reflected in conference themes and newspaper headlines. 'Under-5s prove to have the write stuff' was the headline of a report in the *Times Educational Supplement* in 1999 reporting that 'The number of four-year-olds able to write their names when they start school doubled between 1997 and 1998' (Cassidy 1999). 'A Curriculum for Babies' was a conference theme (RNIB 2000) and a satirical cartoon even appeared in the *Times Educational Supplement* (2000) showing a nurse/doctor handing the new-born baby over to the mother saying 'Congratulations . . . It's an accountant.'

At the same time, there is an acknowledgement that more young children than ever are being identified as exhibiting behaviour problems, even in the less formal environment of the early years settings. In an enquiry undertaken in Western Europe in the early 1980s, among over one hundred university professors, educational psychologists, heads of special schools and researchers, it was found that progressively younger children were showing signs of disruptive behaviour. Respondents recognised that behaviour problems were 'starting to be seen among younger children and thus in primary school and even at the preschool stage' (Lawrence and Steed 1984: 11). In the UK, teachers in primary schools also admitted that behaviour problems start earlier in children's lives (Lawrence and Steed 1986).

Across the Atlantic, the Early Report (2001: 2), quoting Linda Nelson, voices the same concerns when it states that 'the number of children under the age of five with a history of being expelled from multiple child care programs due to challenging behaviours is a growing concern'. In the same vein, Shonkoff and Phillips (2000: 104) state that 'Just 20 years ago, the thought that very young children could manifest serious psychological disorders was unimaginable. Today people recognise that toddlers and preschoolers are subject to many of the same kinds of emotion-related disorders that have long been studied in older children, adolescents and adults.'

A contentious issue?

Some problems do persist for considerable periods of time throughout the preschool years and can prove to be long-lasting if no help is given (Egeland *et al.* 1990; Douglas 1989; Kauffman 1989; Laing 1984; Jenkins *et al.* 1984). In addition to this, children who exhibit problems at an early age tend to exhibit more behaviour problems in later childhood and adulthood than those children who have similar problems but with a later onset (Walker-Hall and Sylva 2001; Clarizio 1990; Lawrence and Steed 1986). Even before young children's behaviour problems started to draw attention (Hughes *et al.* 1979), pointed out that a significant proportion of children who were exhibiting behaviour difficulties on entry to school were still displaying these problems eighteen months later. Such research findings lend weight to arguments that young children's behaviour difficulties and problems should not be ignored.

On the other hand, it is often argued that behaviour problems in young children are common and temporary, and frequently related to developmental and maturational factors in the child (Shonkoff and Phillips 2000; Tibbets *et al.* 1986; Jenkins *et al.* 1984). In this period of major and swift developmental changes, many problems evident in preschoolers, such as tantrums, inattentiveness and aggression, are, to some extent, normative and simply reflect developmental changes, pressures and obstacles (Egeland *et al.* 1990). In addition, the broad range of individual differences makes it difficult to distinguish normal variations from maturational delays and transient from persistent problems (Shonkoff and Phillips 2000). In young children, many behaviour problems arise simply because the children do not yet know what is socially acceptable and what is expected of them. Often, even if children know what behaviours are acceptable or expected, they are not necessarily capable of producing them at this stage (Fontana 1985). Indeed, Douglas (1989) comments that the behaviour problems that many children show in the early years will eventually resolve themselves and disappear. Usually, as children get older and the nursery experience is absorbed, they tend to develop more socially acceptable behaviour patterns (Laing 1984). Such arguments would appear to support the practice of ignoring behaviours considered to be unusual or different from the norm. But is this enough?

What behaviours are of concern in the early years?

In the case of young children, it is far from easy to distinguish between those difficulties which are of a temporary nature and those which may have more lasting effect. As the case studies outlined below illustrate, the question is what behaviours should be of concern during the early years?

Case study 1: Tony in the nursery class

Tony is four years and three months old and he attends a nursery class for a second year. He is a clever, intelligent and exceptionally creative boy. He is also the 'clown' of the class. Against all the teacher's efforts, Tony's behaviour remains a challenge for her, the other staff and the children in the nursery. Tony always finishes his work quickly, without completing it. When the nursery teacher, Mrs Rose, encourages him to look at his work again and make some effort, he replies that he has finished and his work is good. He then starts wandering from one working group to another making faces and gestures and causing laughter and much excitement. Mrs Rose has repeatedly tried to discourage him from this kind of behaviour either by talking to him and reasoning with him or, on some occasions, by telling him off and threatening to punish him if he will not stop. Nothing seems to work with Tony.

Case study 2: Angelica in the nursery class

Angelica is four and half years old and she has attended the nursery class, run at the church hall, for almost six months now. Angelica has good social and language skills that are evident to all members of staff and visitors. Recently, some children have been complaining that Angelica takes their toys and spoils their play. She hits, beats and bites them. The nursery teacher, Mrs Wright, herself witnessed such behaviour on two occasions. In the first instance, Angelica was trying to take some toys from Maria, another girl in the nursery class. When Maria protested and refused to give the toys, Angelica scratched her on the face and ran away with the toys. On the second occasion, Angelica wanted the tricycle which Jack, a boy from the class, was riding. Jack refused to give up the tricycle and Angelica pushed him. Jack fell on the concrete playground and hurt his leg. On both occasions, Mrs Wright told Angelica off and warned her that next time she behaved like that she would punish her. Angelica apologized and promised not to do it again. Her behaviour, however, did not change.

Mrs Wright has also observed that, recently, Angelica avoids doing or completing any of the activities set out. She often withdraws to the home corner, playing on her own, or sits in the book corner looking at and reading picture books.

Case study 3: George and Annie in the reception class

George is four and a half years old and he attends the reception class at the local primary school. Recently, Mrs Smith, George's mum, visited the class teacher to express her concerns about George's unwillingness to attend the school. Since December (it is now the end of January), almost every morning, George has been complaining that he does not feel well. But the few times Mrs Smith gave in and kept George

continued on facing page

at home he was OK. After long conversations with George, Mrs Smith came to think that he might have been having trouble with Annie. Annie called him names such as 'baby', 'ugly' and 'chimpanzee'. She spoiled his snack and, a few times, she had taken some of the toys that George used to take with him to share with his friends.

The class teacher, Mrs Proctor, seemed surprised. She said that Annie is a well-behaved and articulate girl with good manners and social skills. She couldn't see why Annie should have taken George's snack. She always had her own. As for the toys, Mrs Proctor said that, by now, all parents and children should know that nobody is allowed to bring toys or other stuff from home, because of the problems, like these, that are created. Mrs Proctor said that she was sorry about the way George felt. She did not, actually, notice any problems. He is a quiet and well-mannered boy and he seems to get on well with all children. As far as she knows, he has never caused any trouble or been involved in trouble. He is actually so quiet that she sometimes forgets that he is in the classroom.

Mrs Proctor thanked Mrs Smith for sharing her concerns and she promised to look at the situation to find out exactly what is happening.

Case study 4: James in the reception class

James is four years and three months old and he has attended the reception class in the local school since September (it is now mid-November). He is an affectionate boy and plays well with all children. He seems to get on especially well with the girls, with whom he spends most of the free-play time in the home corner. He likes playing with soft toys and dolls. Because of this, some children call him names such as 'baby' and 'girly'. On these occasions Mrs MacNab tells the children off by reminding them that name-calling is not allowed in the school. James ignores the name-calling and he seems not to be upset.

continued on next page

James is often clumsy and has some difficulties in walking and running. The rest of the children seem to avoid including him in their play and games, especially when they are outdoors. James, however, shows much perseverance in 'including himself' in the play, although peripherally. When play is not going well, he is always the one to be blamed. The other children 'punish' him by excluding him from the game. However, his punishment lasts just a few minutes. He keeps going back asking the children to let him join the game again.

The other children are complaining to the teacher that James has been naughty and spoils their play. The teacher discreetly interfered to resolve the problem by guiding and advising both James and the other children. She was not sure whether this was the right thing to do, though. She believes that the children should be given the opportunity to resolve their differences on their own. In addition, she felt that she was imposing James's presence on to other children. But she felt for him being always blamed. It was not his fault that he was not doing well in physical activities. And, anyway, he is such a good-natured child.

Every morning, James arrives at school accompanied by his mother, Mrs Todd. Throughout the school-day, Mrs Todd spends her time in her car parked outside the school. From the early days, Mrs McNab tried to suggest to Mrs Todd, in a discreet manner, that there was no need to stay there any more. She reassured her that, even from the first days, James had adjusted well in the school. Mrs Todd replied that she needed to be there in case James needs her.

Recently, however, Mrs MacNab started to be concerned about James's change of behaviour. He spends most of his time in the home corner playing on his own. Often he stands on the chair to see whether his mother is outside. On a few occasions he started crying, saying that he wanted to go home. During the outdoors playtime, he has stopped making any effort to join the other children. He spends most of his time with his mother.

Case study 5: Tina in Year 1

Tina is five years old and has attended Year 1 in the local primary school for almost six months now. In contrast with other children she seems not to have adjusted to the class environment and routine. She is always the last to follow the teacher's instructions and guidance with regard to planned activities. She always finds something else to do, such as tidying up the home and book corner, picking up any toys and games left on the floor, cleaning up the tables, sharpening the pencils and colour pens. It often takes the teacher's personal invitation for her to respond. Usually, in these instances the teacher invites her to join the group and sit next to her.

During story time and group discussions, Tina constantly interrupts the teacher and the other children to answer questions or make suggestions. She indicates, although politely, that she knows the story and what will happen next. She often takes over from the teacher, either carrying on with the story or, if she does not know the story, by developing it as she likes, often blending it with her life's events. During activities set up by the teacher, Tina is constantly asking for the teacher's help. The teacher, Mrs Green, usually responds by helping and encouraging her to continue her work. If Mrs Green does not respond, Tina either complains that she does not know what to do and how to do it, or asks the teacher to check whether she has done her work well.

Tina is a pleasant girl with good language and communication skills and seems to do well in all activities. Mrs Green is always positive with her, but she feels that Tina takes a lot of her time and that is not fair for some of the other children who often need her help and support more. During free-play, Tina is often wandering around, not concentrating on any particular activities. She usually ends up talking to other members of staff. All the staff like her and even spoil her with their attention. She is a much liked child and they find it difficult to be strict with her.

Case study 6: Rory in Year 1

Rory has been attending the Year 1 class since September. By mid-November the teacher, Mrs Tucker, felt that she had exhausted all her energy and understanding as well as all her management skills dealing with Rory's behaviour. Rory never sits in one place. He jumps on the tables, chairs and the windowsill and a few times he has hurt himself seriously. He jumps on to other children, kicks and destroys their construction games, snatches their work and rips it up. When he is told off or has 'time-off' he starts swearing at both the staff and the other children. Using the colouring pens, he had scribbled all over the walls and, on one occasion, he took the paints and painted the toilets. The school had to redecorate them. When he is at the height of his disruptive behaviour, the children laugh with him, something which seems to make things worse. However, all the children avoid him and no one likes to sit next to him. The few moments Rory is calm, he is usually sitting on his own.

Mrs Tucker spoke to Rory's mother who said that Rory was out of control at home as well. She cannot do anything. She commented, 'I take it at home, the teacher has to take it at the school.'

Activity 1a

Choose any one of the case studies or, if you like, follow all of them:

i.   Consider whether the case(s) would have concerned you.
ii. Identify specific behaviours of concern.
iii. Explain why these behaviours would concern you.

The early years practitioners' and teachers' points of view

In Tony's case, his behaviour certainly did concern Mrs Rose, the nursery teacher. Tony had been in the nursery school for a second year and Mrs Rose was expecting him (i) to have adjusted to the nursery class environment and routine and (ii) to have developed skills and abilities appropriate for his developmental stage and his perceived potential. In contrast, Tony's behaviour seemed to be an obstacle that interfered as much with his own learning and development as with the other children's learning. Tony is an intelligent and extremely creative boy, a real 'spark', but Mrs Rose could not take any more of this behaviour. His work was far behind the work of other children and she was concerned that he would have great difficulties the following year, in the more formal learning environment of Year 1.

Mrs Wright found Angelica's behaviour very puzzling. She was sometimes very aggressive and at other times withdrawn and isolated. There were increasing complaints from the other children who seemed to avoid her. Mrs Wright could not understand how a child like Angelica with good social and language skills could not make any friends. Actually, thinking about it, it seemed that Angelica had not established any close friendships with any of the children.

To start with, Mrs Proctor had no concerns at all about either George or Annie. Even when Mrs Smith spoke to her, Mrs Proctor thought that it was probably one of those fights 'over possession' and difficulties in sharing the same toys and play equipment. She felt, however, that she could not ignore George's expressed feelings. She decided to speak to both children in her own time and find out what was happening. At some point, she organised group activities and made arrangements for George and Annie to work alongside each other. She joined them and starting talking about their experiences in the school and whether they liked it. Annie was talkative, but George said nothing. Mrs Proctor asked Annie whether she had taken any of George's toys and whether she accidentally hurt him. Annie started crying, saying that that was a lie. She said that she also had the same toys as George, because she had two brothers. George, on the other hand, said nothing. He was tense and kept his head down, biting his lips and not making any eye contact. Mrs Proctor felt that she did not handle the situation well, but she also thought that George was probably 'making up' stories. Did he want to attract his mother's attention? Mrs Proctor was not clear what to do next, but she decided to follow the issue further.

Although James's behaviour often caused complaints by the other children, Mrs MacNab was hardly concerned about this. She started to be worried, however, when James became gradually withdrawn and weepy. Mrs MacNab thought that Mrs Todd's insistence on remaining outside the school had not helped him. It seemed that he had become more attached to his mother now than he had seemed to be when he first arrived in the school. Mrs MacNab once again tried to discourage Mrs Todd from remaining outside the school, but on this occasion Mrs Todd was adamant that she would not go anywhere. She said that she was concerned that James was recently becoming easily upset and she did not want to upset him further by not being there.

Talking about Tina, Mrs Green said that she would not say that Tina displayed any behaviour problems. Her behaviour, however, became problematic in the classroom context. Tina was constantly seeking for her attention and, in a way, she seemed to lack any confidence to do anything on her own. This was in sharp contrast with the confidence which she showed when she was talking to adults. Tina was a polite and much liked child and often Mrs Green found it difficult to be strict with her. She did not like to hurt her feelings. However, Tina's attempts to monopolise the teacher's attention became tiring, deprived the other children of equal attention and interfered with the learning and teaching process.

Mrs Tucker, referring to Rory's behaviour, described it as being hyperactive, aggressive, hostile and disruptive. She said that she was concerned as much for his safety and well-being as for that of the other children. His behaviour affected not only his own learning, but the learning of the other children. Mrs Tucker said that she needed constantly to keep an eye on him, because she did not know what he would do next. During the last month, the Learning Support Assistant (LSA) had worked closely with him, but she felt deeply demoralised by her inability to make any difference to his behaviour. Neither positive reinforcement nor punishment worked with him. Reasoning with him and counselling seemed to be a waste of words, energy and time. In addition, there was no hope for any understanding, support or help from his family.

The cases described above and the views expressed by the early years practitioners highlight the difficulties surrounding the conceptualisation and identification of behaviour problems in the early years. There are cases that immediately raise concerns (as with Rory) and others that may not be identified, unless something happens to bring the issue to professionals' attention (as in George's and Annie's cases) or the child's behaviour becomes puzzling (as in Angelica's case). In a number of cases, the behaviours go unnoticed, or ignored, because they are not considered problematic in the first instance or they are not considered serious enough to be dealt with (as in Tony's, Tina's and James's cases). However, in the end, in all cases the early years practitioners and teachers acknowledged the behaviour problems illustrated in the case studies on the basis of the following variables: (i) the behaviour had an impact on individual children's feelings, well-being and learning, (ii) the behaviour had an impact on the other children's physical safety, well-being and learning, and (iii) the behaviour interfered with the learning process and the work done in the setting.

Despite the difficulties illustrated in the case studies, the early identification of children's behaviour problems followed by appropriate assessment and intervention is acknowledged as a step that is necessary in order to prevent the escalation of problems (Jenkins *et al.* 1984; Chazan *et al.* 1991).

Concluding remarks

There is increasing concern about the rising numbers of behaviour problems reported among young children, but difficulties exist in distinguishing transient and developmental behaviour problems from those which may have a long-lasting effect. In addition, the prognosis for the continuity or discontinuity of these problems is less clear. However, early years practitioners' and teachers' perceptions of young children's behaviour suggest that any behaviour that has an effect on the child's own and other children's well-being and on the teaching and learning processes should receive due attention to eliminate future difficulties.

Activity 1b

i. Do you think that the case study practitioners' identification criteria are useful?
ii. Could only one of the criteria be used?

Chapter 2

The nature and extent of behaviour problems in the early years

The nature of behaviour problems in young children

Research has shown that specific problem behaviours are age related (Egeland *et al.* 1990; Links 1983). Young children tend to have a greater number of extreme scores on such behaviours as overactivity, restlessness, fighting, clumsiness, teasing others, destructiveness, lack of concentration, attention-seeking, speech difficulties, tension, shyness, extreme timidity and temper tantrums (Papatheodorou 1995; Luk *et al.* 1991; Golding and Rush 1986). Aggressive behaviour towards peers is a common complaint in pre-schoolers. Active and boisterous children tend to show domineering behaviour and become more aggressive and less popular with their peers (Campbell 1983). However, most acts of aggression among young children have to do with fights over possession or property (Sutton-Smith *et al.* 1988; Campbell 1983); aggressive acts are often observed when a child aims to attain or retrieve some object or privilege from his/her peers (Biehler 1981). In this sense, most preschoolers' aggression is instrumental rather than hostile, intending to hurt other children.

Young children's problem behaviours are often understood as transient developmental phenomena which, according to Mac-Farlane *et al.* (1962: 153), are 'trial-and-error problem-solving attempts to meet new and/or ambiguous pressure, social and bio-logical, external and internal'. Between the ages of three and five years temper tantrums and destructive behaviours reflect expressive and adaptive patterns in new situations, negativism and resistance become coping mechanisms, while fears, timidity and excessive dependence are signs of a need for protection (MacFarlane *et al.* 1962). However, the universality of the symptomatic behaviour reported in young children seems to explain the fact that adults tend to perceive these behaviours as less problematic than the same behaviours exhibited by older children (Campbell 1983; Luk *et al.* 1991). Children's perceived level of development appears to influence to a large extent how particular behaviours are perceived, interpreted and labelled by adults.

Gender and type of behaviour problem

Studies undertaken among preschoolers have also shown that, in general, boys tend to show more acting out behaviours, whereas girls tend to be more withdrawn, indicating that the nature of behaviour problems is also gender-related. For example, Richman *et al.*'s (1975) study revealed that boys were significantly more overactive, while girls were fearful. The researchers commented that, although there was no significant difference between the sexes in overall scores, significant sex differences in relation to individual items were identified. Similarly, Laing (1984) reported that more boys than girls were seen as aggressive and/or overactive, whereas there were no gender differences in withdrawn and/or dependent behaviours. Finally, McGuire and Richman (1986a) identified more boys than girls (a ratio 2:1) as having marked difficulties with respect to conduct problems, high activity and attention-seeking, while in the case of social maladjustment, McGhee and Short (1991) identified twice as many males as females. A significant association between the child's sex and the category of behaviour was also reported by McGee *et al.* (1984) who found a significant sex difference in the antisocial grouping but no significant differences in the neurotic grouping. The author's own study has also revealed a similar trend (Papatheodorou 1995).

Aggressive behaviour: a gender issue?

There is a degree of disagreement among psychologists regarding the factors responsible for gender differences in aggression; some psychologists advocate that differences are produced by socialisation, while others stress attention to biology (Fishbein 1984). It is common to attribute behavioural differences in boys and girls to learned sex roles (Fontana 1985; Stott *et al.* 1975). Children learn what is expected of them as boys or girls, and tend to hold increasingly to these stereotypes as they grow older.

Other researchers seem to suggest that the tendency of children to show different types of behaviour may reflect temperamental differences. Fishbein (1984: 181), reviewing a number of cross-cultural studies, states that:

> If boys are everywhere more aggressive on average than girls, it is difficult to argue that different patterns of socialization produce the aggression differences. Each culture has unique ways of socializing children, and if boys are found to be more aggressive, support is gained for a biological basis.

Thomas and Chess (1977, 1984), in their seminal New York longitudinal study, followed three groups of infants with different temperamental dimensions (that is, 'easy', 'difficult' and the 'slow-to-warm-up') through into later childhood and found that their behaviour remained remarkably constant. However, they point out that their findings 'do not imply that temperament is *always* a significant variable in the ontogenesis and course of *every* behaviour disorder' (Thomas and Chess 1977: 41). They explain that, in some instances, temperament may play a crucial role; in other cases it may be somewhat influential, and in other instances it may play a minor or even insignificant role. It is rather the interaction process with the care givers that determines the final outcome. In a similar vein, Graham *et al.* (1973) comment on the link between adverse temperament and adverse family attitudes and, possibly, relationships. Fishbein (1984: 182) also endorses this view by stating that:

> It is likely that there is a biological basis for sex differences in aggression. In early childhood there is great overlap between boys' and girls' expression, but the most aggressive children are more typically boys. As children mature, different socialization pressures operate on them that reinforce and exaggerate these biological tendencies.

Temperamental differences then are likely to elicit reinforcement from the environment and therefore to be quickly overlaid by learned characteristics. Even in a child's first months of life, parents tend to show subtle differences in their behaviour towards the two sexes (Fontana 1988; Clark 1986).

Gender and seriousness of behaviour problems

The overall pattern is that more boys than girls show extreme behaviours, especially in the more severe category (Laing 1984; Stott *et al.* 1975; Davie *et al.* 1972). Laing (1984), in her study among preschoolers, reports a ratio 4:1 of boys to girls as having serious behaviour difficulties, whereas the numbers of boys and girls were fairly even in the whole group and in the 'some difficulties' category. Similarly, Borg and Falzon (1989, 1990) also found gender to be a significant moderator of teachers' perceptions of the seriousness of specific behaviours. The same behaviours may be judged as more serious depending on the child's gender. For example, being unorganised and untidy may be judged as a more serious problem when exhibited by girls, while being talkative or fearful is considered more serious when shown by boys.

The extent of behaviour problems in young children

The prevalence rates of behaviour problems in the early years are usually inferred from the prevalence rates revealed in studies undertaken among children attending compulsory education and cover the ages four to eight. Table 2.1 summarises the prevalence rates of behaviour problems revealed by some studies, undertaken in the UK, Europe and across the Atlantic, which reveal a divergent picture. Studies undertaken exclusively among preschool and reception class children have also revealed diverse prevalence rates (Table 2.2). Laing (1984), in her study among preschoolers, reported 38.3 per cent of the whole sample as presenting behavioural difficulties of varying degrees of severity. Of those, 10.6 per cent exhibited 'serious' difficulties and 27.7 per cent had 'some' difficulties.

McGuire and Richman's (1986a) study, undertaken among preschoolers, reported different prevalence figures among pre-schoolers who attended different early years provision settings, that is, playgroups, nursery classes in schools and day nurseries. The playgroup sample had the smallest percentage (3.3 per cent) of children 'at risk', followed by the nursery classes in schools

Table 2.1 The extent of behaviour problems in general studies which have included ages four to eight.

Study	Extent of behaviour problems
McGee *et al.* (1984) (New Zealand)	9.0
Baker *et al.* (1985) (UK)	10.3
Wheldall and Merrett (1988) (UK)	16.0
McGhee and Short (1991) (USA)	12.0

(10.8 per cent). In the day nurseries substantially more children were identified with problems (that is, 34.9 per cent) than in the other two settings.

St James-Roberts *et al.*'s (1994) study undertaken among reception class children revealed 15 to 21 per cent of children as having both behavioural and emotional problems. Luk *et al.* (1991), using McGuire's Behaviour Problem Checklist (BPCL) among Hong Kong preschool children (three to four years old), reported 27.5 per cent of children as being perceived to exhibit behaviour problems. The author's own study, undertaken in Greece, revealed that 14.3 per cent of young children (four to six years old) attending nursery classes were perceived to exhibit behaviour problems. Of these, 2.1 per cent were judged as being very serious and the figure increased to 5.8 per cent when problems judged to be serious were taken into account (Papatheodorou 1995).

Table 2.2 The extent of behaviour problems among preschoolers.

Study	Seriousness of behaviour problems		
	Serious %	Moderate %	Mild/minor %
Richman *et al.* (1975, 1982)	1.1	6.2	15
Jenkins *et al.* (1984)	19–29 (tantrums and management problems)		
Laing (1984)	10.6	27.7	38.3
McGuire and Richman (1986a)	3.3–34.9 (depending on the EYs setting)		
St. James-Roberts *et al.* (1994)	15 to 21 (overall rate)		
Luk *et al.* (1991)	27.5 (overall rate)		
Papatheodorou (1995)	2.1	5.8	14.3

A similarly divergent picture of prevalence figures has been reported by studies undertaken among preschoolers' parents. Richman *et al.*'s (1975, 1982) studies, undertaken among three-year-old children, revealed that 7 per cent of children had a problem which was considered by parents to be moderate to severe (6.2 per cent and 1.1 per cent, respectively), while a further 15 per cent had mild behaviour problems. Similarly, Jenkins *et al.* (1984), interviewing the parents of children aged 2 to $4\frac{1}{2}$ years, found that, at all ages, between 19 and 29 per cent of children displayed frequent tantrums and were difficult to manage.

While individual studies show variations in the extent of behaviour problems among young children, overall trends seem to reveal up to 3 per cent of young children as exhibiting severe behaviour problems. This figure may rise to 7 per cent if children with moderately severe difficulties are included, and if pupils with mild problems are counted, the incidence figure rises to 20 to 30 per cent and even 50 per cent, in some cases. In general, research findings show greater consistency in the reported prevalence rates of problem behaviours regarded as being serious, but the figures are more variable for behaviours considered as being of moderate or mild seriousness. Most importantly, the reported figures regarding mild and not very serious problem behaviours show the role which personal and professional characteristics and levels of tolerance may play in their identification. Of course, the reported figures show variation depending on (i) the setting where the children are and (ii) who is reporting on children's behaviour, that is, parents or early years practitioners.

Age and the extent of behaviour problems

Most of the studies report that younger children far exceed older children in the number of exhibited behaviour problems. Laing (1984) reported that the number of children with difficulties was greater in the young age group (three- to four-year-olds) than in the older group (four- to five-year-olds): there were nearly twice as many younger children as older children exhibiting behaviour problems. She argues that the initial adjustment of a group of children in a new setting is a possible cause of problems; the three-year-olds go through a transitional stage (from infancy to childhood) that requires them to make new adjustments. McGhee and Short (1991) also found the highest prevalence of social mal-adjustment at the kindergarten level, followed by a considerable drop at first grade. They observe that the high prevalence of mal-adjustment in kindergarten level may be due to children's under-socialisation and to transition from one setting to another.

Gender and the extent of behaviour problems

Gender is another variable that has frequently been considered in assessing the extent of behaviour problems: it is suggested that boys tend to have higher prevalence rates of behaviour problems than girls. Most studies have consistently reported a ratio of 2 and 3, and in some cases even 4 and 5, boys to 1 girl as exhibiting behaviour problems (Wheldall and Merrett 1988; Shea and Bauer 1987; Davie *et al.* 1972). These differences seem to diminish among preschoolers, although boys are still perceived to be signi-ficantly less well adjusted than girls (Davies and Brember 1991; Jenkins *et al.* 1980).

Why the different prevalence rates?

To estimate the prevalence of behaviour problems is not an easy task (Baker *et al.* 1985). Definitions and criteria that are used, methodological issues and policy and economic factors all contri-bute to the nature and prevalence of identified problems (Kauff-man 1989; Zabel 1988a; Smith *et al.* 1988; Kavale *et al.* 1986; Links 1983).

Definition of behaviour problems

As has been discussed in Chapter 1, what constitutes problem behaviour in young children is a contentious issue. If the defini-tions of behaviour problems are not clear and precise, then the number of children identified as exhibiting behaviour problems cannot be determined accurately or reliably (Kauffman 1989). Links (1983), reviewing sixteen major community surveys, states that few definitive conclusions could be drawn because each of the surveys differed in terms of definitions used for behaviour problems. Similarly, other researchers reviewing a number of studies found nearly fifty terms used to define behaviour problems.

To name a few, such terms include emotional disturbance, behaviour problem, behaviour disorder, behaviour disability, conduct problem, conduct disorder, maladjustment, disruptive, aggressive, non-compliant and delinquent behaviours (Kavale *et al.* 1986; Wood and Lakin 1982).

To make things more complicated, the use of these terms is also inconsistent. Professionals from different disciplines tend to use different terms for similar conditions or similar terms for different conditions (Upton 1983). John Visser (2002: 69) points out that the field 'is littered with terms, such as "delinquent", "challenging", "disaffected", "phobic", "disturbed", which each of us believes has a meaning shared by colleagues. This is a dangerous assumption to make even between members of the same professional agency.' Main factors which contribute to such diversity and inconsistent use of terminology include:

i.   *the theoretical perspectives* available to conceptualise behaviour problems;
ii. *the different training* of professionals from different disciplines;
iii. *the range of situations* in which professionals encounter children exhibiting behaviour problems;
iv. *the problems associated with the assessment process* and the way in which intervention might be planned;
     (McLoughlin and Lewis 1986; Upton 1983; Epstein *et al.* 1977)

This situation reveals the difficulties which professionals from different, and even the same, disciplines face in communicating among themselves with regard to children's behaviour problems. Often the processes of identification of, and intervention for, children's behaviour problems start on the assumption that all involved parties share the meaning of the terms used. The wide range of terms and the different definitions that exist indicate that this is not always the case. It then becomes important that professionals communicating between themselves about individual children acknowledge explicitly the terms which they use, examine their definitions and provide, if necessary, an operational definition which they will use in the identification and intervention process. This will enable them to communicate effectively among themselves and serve the child in the best way.

Methodological issues

Methods and procedures that are used to select the study samples lead to diverse prevalence rates (Smith *et al.* 1988). Different numbers are likely to be obtained depending on how the sample is selected. Social class, age, gender biases and differences in the geographical location of the population may also influence the prevalence rates (Kauffman 1989). The instruments which are used (e.g. questionnaires, interviews, observation), the kind of questions that are asked and the way the level of problem severity is defined or determined will also affect the reported prevalence rates. Finally, who gathers the data (e.g. a researcher, policy-maker, teacher, psychologist etc) and from whom (parents, teachers, children, etc) may also influence the estimation of the prevalence figures (Campbell 1989; McGee *et al.* 1984; Clarizio and McCoy 1983).

Personal and professional attitudes

Even when the same definitions and methodologies are used, estimates of prevalence may still differ (Kauffman 1989). One of the important variables that affects the definition of behaviour problems is that of teachers' (and early years practitioners') attitudes, perceptions, feelings and degree of tolerance (Galloway 1995). Usually, these people who work directly with children and have the responsibility for their education and care are a major source of information about children's behaviour and often constitute the main referral agencies by acting on the basis of their own judgement (Gavrilidou *et al.* 1993; Jenkins *et al.* 1980; Rubin and Balow 1978). Accordingly, their definition and interpretation of children's behaviour within their settings or class are of great importance in the study of behaviour problems.

Behaviour is often ambiguous and social psychology teaches that the way in which it is interpreted is highly influenced by people's attitudes (Rajecki 1990). 'Attitudes determine for each individual what he will see and hear, what he will think and what he will do' (Allport 1973: 22). They have an evaluative character which prompts individuals to intentionally classify stimuli, in this case children's behaviour, into response categories such as good, disturbing, aggressive etc. Attitudes are seen as the cause and behaviour as the effect (Rajecki 1990; Phillips 1986) so that the same behaviour can be differently perceived and categorised according to the attitudes of the observer.

In educational settings, early years practitioners' and teachers' attitudes play a key role in defining children's behaviour as inappropriate. According to Leach (1977: 191), teachers share many similarities 'by virtue of their shared experience, knowledge and concerns'. The views held within the education culture, in general, and within an individual school in particular, and the teachers' common views of the educational aims and their role constitute the main points of reference for the teacher in defining behaviour problems (Rogers 1982; Doney 1977).

In addition, teachers bring into practice their own subjective definitions of behaviour problems. Individual teachers' views of classroom rules, behavioural expectancies, values and philosophies, both personal and educational, and theoretical knowledge of child behaviour, learning and teaching also affect their perception of what constitutes 'normal', 'good' or 'ideal' behaviour and what are the 'bad' consequences of certain types of behaviour (Lawrence and Steed 1984; Paul 1982; Leach 1977; Hargreaves 1975). In this context Ouay (1986: 53) points out that 'how broadly or narrowly a disorder is defined, how reliable and valid the methods are for assessing the presence of the disorder, and what segment of the population is assessed will drastically influence the number of cases reported'.

Continuity and discontinuity of behaviour problems over time

Age-related specific behaviours are expected to be short-lived and show a decreasing tendency as children grow older. However, several follow-up studies have shown that preschoolers' behaviour problems are identifiable and indicative of some risk of later problems (Links 1983). For example, Manning et al. (1978) found that the group of preschoolers (three- to five-year-olds) who were not well-adjusted in the nursery remained so at the ages of seven and eight years, whereas those children who seemed socially well adjusted showed no signs of behavioural disturbance. Richman et al. (1982) also found that the group of children exhibiting behaviour problems at the age of four continued to display similar behaviour at the age of eight years. McGee et al. (1984) reported that for about 12 per cent of the seven-year-olds who had significant behaviour problems, their problems dated at least from the age of five. Egeland *et al.* (1990) also found that children who displayed behaviour problems in preschool were more likely to have behaviour problems later in the school. That was true especially for acting-out children and, to a lesser degree, for those who were withdrawn. These findings clearly show that there is a trend for behaviour problems to remain stable, at least for some children, over a period of time. Therefore, the study of behaviour problems in the early years becomes an important area for all practitioners involved in children's education and well-being.

Concluding remarks

Research findings have shown that behaviour problems are age- and gender-related with boys being identified as exhibiting more problems and especially of aggressive nature. Temperament has been often seen as an underlying factor, but the interactional process seems to be acknowledged as a determining factor for such problems. With regard to the extent of behaviour problems, research findings have shown greater consistency among the prevalence rates reported for serious than for mild or not very serious problems. This may reflect variations in the definition of behaviour problems, methodological issues and the attitudes of those who make judgements about, and report, behaviour problems. A lack of agreement is also evident regarding the extent to which behaviour problems continue as children grow older. The overall argument is that although some problem behaviours may disappear with time, there is convincing evidence that in many cases the early onset of problem behaviour poses a threat to future well-being and adjustment.

Activity 2

> You may like to work with a colleague and consider:
>
> i.   the nature and extent and seriousness of behaviour prob-
>   lems in your settings;
> ii. whether these behaviour are age- and gender-related;
> iii. personal and professional experiences which have influ-
>   enced the way you understand children's behaviour.

Chapter 3

Definition of behaviour problems

As there is a great variation in terminology, there is also a variety of definitions used for such terminology. It appears that there is not a universal definition about behaviour problems that satisfies professionals who work with children in different capacities (e.g. as children's parents/carers/guardians, teachers, social workers, psychologists, clinicians, lawyers and judges). In fact, individuals and professionals rely on different criteria to define behaviour problems (Visser 2002; Upton 1983).

The lack of consensus concerning the definition of behaviour problems highlights the complexity and difficulties encountered in the identification of behaviour problems and the planning for intervention. It is important that definitions introduced (i) serve the purposes for which professionals use them (e.g. to identify children exhibiting behaviour problems, distinguish those who will receive support within the setting or be referred for further assessment), (ii) inform intervention planning and how such intervention will be implemented, (iii) inform the decisions made by legislative, administrative and advocacy groups with regard to children and the field of behaviour problems and (iv) contribute to continuing research effort to develop new knowledge, theoretical perspectives and practice (Kauffman 1989; Epstein *et al.* 1977).

Within this context, definitions have been classified into three types, that is, 'administrative', 'authoritative' and 'research' definitions. The 'administrative' definitions are those found in rules, regulations and policy documents produced by official bodies. These definitions primarily guide the delivery of services and resources made available. The 'authoritative' definitions attempt to offer an interpretation of behaviour problems according to some particular point of view or theoretical framework. The 'research' definitions set out the parameters which intend to identify the population to which the research results may be relevant or applicable (Cullinan and Epstein 1982; Epstein *et al.* 1977).

Professionals are usually required to operate within the framework indicated in 'administrative' definitions provided in policy documents. However, these definitions are still subject to individual or collective (an agency's committee's or board's) interpretations, especially when they have been vaguely worded. Usually, the different theoretical perspectives that professionals are familiar with, because of their training or professional duties and responsibilities and personal attitudes and values, will guide the interpretation of these definitions. Therefore, 'authoritative' and 'research' definitions should be considered in order to obtain an informed and externally validated interpretation of 'administrative' definitions.

The definition of some terms, used in administrative policies and documents and widely used by professionals, will be discussed from an authoritative perspective and in the light of relevant research to illuminate their theoretical bases. The definitions will be discussed in the light of the major theoretical perspectives which have influenced the educational landscape over the last fifty years. These include the psychoeducational model, the behavioural model, the labelling or interactionist approach and the ecosystemic approach.

The psychoeducational model

The psychoeducational model emphasises the deep and complex roots of behaviour problems (Harden *et al.* 2003) and it is based on the principles of the biogenetic and psychodynamic theories which imply that the problem resides within the individual, either in the soma (body) (biogenetic theory) or in the psyche (psychodynamic theory), or in both psyche and soma (Rhodes 1974). The biogenetic theories understand and explain the development of behaviour problems in terms of individuals' biological makeup, conditions and deviations (Sagor 1974). The psychodynamic theory interprets overt behaviour and, especially, behaviour problems as being the visible symptoms of internal, invisible and unconscious impulses and conflicts whose basic configuration is set both by an inherited biological disposition and by critical events and experiences (social, cultural and family) during the first years of life (Weiss 2002a; Bronson 2000; Davie 1986; Rezmierski and Kotre 1974). Both theories represent the medical paradigm that is also known as the disability paradigm of emotional disturbance (Rhodes 1974). The underlying principles of the psychoeducational model are reflected in terms such as 'mental illness', 'maladjustment' and 'serious emotional difficulties'.

Mental illness – mental health

At the beginning of the twentieth century and until the 1940s, the term 'mental illness' had been widely used in educational settings to refer to children's behaviour problems. The term implied that the child is sick and is suffering from some form of illness that prevents normal adjustment (Upton 1983; Kauffman 1982; Woolfe 1981). Many authors have questioned the value of an illness model. Szasz (1972) argued that the notion of mental illness served to obscure the real problem, which is individuals' continuous struggle against conflicts in relationships and a search for human values. He argued that mental illness had to do with personal, social problems and ethical dilemmas of living, not genetic or psychic states. In the 1940s the use of the term 'mental illness' in educational settings was seriously questioned as it did not provide clear and specific definitions which related directly to classroom practice (Paul 1982; Samuels 1981).

Currently, the term 'mental health' has been introduced to define, in line with Szasz's (1972) earlier arguments about mental illness, a state of well-being in which individuals realise their own abilities and are able to deal with everyday normal stresses of life and can work productively and fruitfully. Weare and Gray (2003: 18) state that the term mental health is used to refer to a state of 'positive wellness' as well as to 'determinants' of such a state. The term does not assume that individuals are in static states, but focuses on learning that utilises emotional and social competencies.

Maladjustment

In 1944, in Britain, the term 'maladjustment' was introduced to refer to those pupils 'who show evidence of emotional instability and psychological disturbance and require special educational treatment in order to effect their personal, social or educational readjustment' (cited in DES 1955: 22). Again, although the term was not expressed in clinical terms, still it was considered to be vague and unable to provide exact criteria for identifying behaviour problems and the provision needed (Galloway and Goodwin 1987; DES 1955). It was concerned only with those children whose problems were severe enough for them to receive specialised help and it did not take into account those less serious, although far more frequent, cases, as well as failing to deal with maladjustment at an early stage, before any disturbance became deep-rooted (Lovell 1958; DES 1955). It took little or no account of the individual circumstances and the context in which a child was identified and labelled as being maladjusted (Woolfe 1981). It assumed a permanent condition, which might unnecessarily stigmatise the child and it was confined to children who could be identified within the educational system; it also ignored very young children and older children outside the educational system (DES 1955, 1978). Although the term maladjustment was broader in context, its focus still remained on the individual child.

Chazan (1963, 1970), while acknowledging the weaknesses of the term, states its merits. He points out that the term suggests that children's problems are seen mainly as reactions to educational strains and stresses. It avoids giving the impression that a child with difficulties in socio-emotional development is necessarily behaving 'abnormally' or is 'ill'. He claimed that the term 'gives the widest possible scope for appropriate help to be given to children in need of it' (Chazan 1963: 29). Galloway and Goodwin (1987) agree with that latter statement, but argue that maladjustment might be used to describe any behaviour which teachers find disturbing, so that children might be removed from the school. Although there was no agreement on the definition of the term, 'maladjustment' had been broadly used in English and European literature until 1981 when the Education Act abolished the category model of special educational needs.

Emotional disturbance

In the 1980s, Bower (1982) introduced the term 'emotional disturbance' which was defined in terms of children's learning, interpersonal relationships, behaviour and the development of illnesses and phobias. He claimed that for emotional disturbance to be acknowledged, children's behaviours should exist to *'a marked degree over a period of time'* (Bower 1982: 57). This definition was used by the US Federal legislation and regulations for special education to refer to 'seriously emotionally disturbed' children, that is, to children who engage in actions that are not easily understood and are explained as being the result of internal conflicts or lack of inner controls.

The term serious emotional disturbance was widely criticised because of the non-inclusion of children who are socially maladjusted, that is, children who show acts of strange, unconventional and deviant behaviour, but who are not emotionally disturbed. However, it has been argued that, although social maladjustment and emotional disturbance are not necessarily synonymous terms, there is a considerable overlap between them (Clarizio 1987; Kirk 1962). In addition, it is important to keep in mind that it is rather difficult to differentiate between socially maladjusted and emotionally disturbed children because although the overt behaviour may seem to be the same, the causes may be quite different (Raiser and Van Nagel 1980). In this context, it has been argued that the criteria and standards for severe emotional disturbance should be broadened to include antisocial, socially maladjusted and conduct-disordered children (Walker *et al.* 1990).

The behavioural model

In contrast to the psychodynamic approach, the behavioural model is concerned with observable behaviour and the ways in which this behaviour is learned rather than with inner mental processes (Harden *et al.* 2003; Kauffman 1989; Davie 1986). Therefore, behaviour problems are defined more in terms of children's learning and less in terms of internal psychological states (Paul 1982). In terms of the learning theories, the behaviour has been understood as (i) being controlled by its consequences and environmental contingencies of reward and punishment and (ii) is learned by observing behaviour and its consequences in other people (Bronson 2000; Porter 2000; Vasta *et al.* 1992; Kauffman 1982; Russ 1974).

The behavioural model does not ignore individuals' thoughts and internal affective states, but these are seen as arising from environmental events (Kauffman 1982). The behavioural model is concerned with what psychodynamic theorists might call 'symptoms' and has introduced the concept of environment as a highly relevant feature in the formulation of such symptomatic behaviour (Davie 1986). Personal variables and genetic endowment are not seen as entities that can make behaviour happen. Instead they are understood in terms of the way environmental events shape them. Terms such as behavioural disorders and emotional and behavioural difficulties reflect the underlying principles of the behavioural model.

Behavioural disorder

In the USA, the dissatisfaction with the term 'emotionally disturbed' led to the introduction of the term 'behavioural disorder' which (i) focuses on symptomatic behaviour and not on the person/child and, therefore, is less stigmatising than the term emotional disturbance and (ii) suggests that individuals have learned to behave in inappropriate ways and, in this way, highlights the educational responsibility (Kauffman 1989; Smith et al. 1988; McLoughlin and Lewis 1986; Wood and Lakin 1982). Behaviour disordered children are seen as being 'unhappy with themselves, unpopular with their peers, and unsuccessful in their school work' (Reeve and Kauffman 1978: 124).

The environmental determinants of behaviour disorders are clearly demonstrated in Kauffman's (1977: 23) definition which states that 'children with behavior disorders are those who chronically and markedly respond to their environment in socially unacceptable and or personally unsatisfying ways, but who can be taught more socially acceptable and personally satisfying behavior'. Still, the term has been criticised as locating the problem behaviour 'within' the child, although the influences are external, and it has been suggested that both the terms 'emotionally disturbed' and 'behaviourally disordered' should be avoided (Reinert and Huang 1987).

Emotional and behavioural difficulties

In the UK, with the publication of the Warnock report (DES 1978) and the consequent Education Act in 1981, the term 'emotional and behavioural difficulties' was introduced in educational contexts. The term reflected a move from unsatisfactory attempts to define emotional disturbance to an emphasis on defining observable behaviour (Williams 1991). Circular 9/94 (DfE 1994: 7) states that 'emotional and behavioural difficulties lie on the continuum between behaviour which challenges teachers but is within normal, albeit unacceptable, bounds and that which is indicative of serious mental illness'. The Circular states that emotional and behavioural difficulties range from social maladaption to abnormal emotional stresses that are persistent and manifest in many different forms and severities of withdrawn, passive, depressive, aggressive or self-injurious tendencies.

Bowman (1990: 198) states that pupils labelled emotionally/ behaviourally difficult have 'unmet affective and social needs which unfavourably mediate learning experiences', while Williams (1991) observes that emotional and behavioural difficulties cover a wide range of psychological problems, ranging from chronic disorders to temporarily troubled behaviour.

Social, emotional and behavioural difficulties

The revised code of practice for SEN (DfES 2001a) has introduced the term 'behavioural, emotional and social difficulties' (BESD) and the 'Social, emotional and Behavioural Difficulties Association (SEBDA) (previously known as the Association of Workers for Children with Emotional and Behavioural Difficulties, AWCEBD) argues for the use of the term 'social, emotional and behavioural difficulties'. Cole (2003: 1), quoting Daniel's and his colleagues' research, points out that 'it is the past and present social and emotional experience of the child interacting with all aspects of the surrounding environment that most commonly explain why the young people behave in the way they do'. Accordingly, he argues that the terms 'social' and 'emotional' should precede 'behavioural' to make the term 'social, emotional and behavioural difficulties' (SEBD) rather than 'behavioural, emotional and social difficulties' (BESD) (Cole 2003: 1).

The labelling theory: the interactionist approach

The psychoeducational and behavioural models are individualised psychological models which place emphasis on the individual child, although the source of the problem is seen as either 'within' or 'outside' the child. However, sociologists and social psychologists argue that (i) any label applied to the child must be understood in the context of the powerful characteristics of the social context and (ii) children's behaviour should be viewed within the context of social interactions and interrelationships (Rhodes 1967). This way of understanding problem behaviour came to be known as the 'labelling theory' or the 'interactionist approach', which are also referred to as the 'deviation' paradigm (Rhodes 1974).

The interactionist approach places emphasis on (i) the interaction processes which may produce normal or deviant behaviour depending on the codes, norms and values of individual cultures, (ii) the way in which behaviour problems are defined and controlled according to those codes, norms and values and (iii) how children's emotional and behavioural problems may constitute exaggerations of, or deviations from, agreed norms rather than being mental illness or disease (Upton and Cooper 1990; Furlong 1985; Hoghuchi 1983; Hargreaves *et al.* 1975).

In this context, the judgement of 'normal' or 'abnormal' behaviour depends upon individual cultural norms and codes which are 'regarded as a set of behavioural expectations, rules or guides, shared by an identifiable social group' (Hoghuchi 1983: 19). Nonconformity or disobedience to, and deviations from, these norms and rules become of concern because they threaten and upset the society's, or any group's, values and sense of order (Hoghuchi 1983; Rutter and Giller 1983). In addition, a clash between the values and expectations of educational systems and the values which children acquire in their own homes and community may result in the identification of certain problem behaviours (Harden *et al.* 2003; Davie *et al.* 1972).

The interactionist approach emphasises the way in which disruptive and disturbing behaviour is reacted to by those in authority, since the reaction to such behaviour has a profound effect on its future development (Furlong 1985). It is claimed that individuals 'are *made* different – that is, socially differentiated – by the process of being seen and treated as different in a system of social practices that crystallizes distinctions between deviant and conventional behavior and persons' (Rains *et al.* 1975: 94). Consequently, problem behaviour and any deviation from the norm is understood as being created by those who make the rules rather than being attributed to an individual's inherent qualities.

The labelling theory shifts the theoretical concern from the question of the aetiology of problem behaviours to the question of how behaviour is controlled and how the label given may systematically reinforce and stabilise certain behaviours among labelled individuals (Rains et al. 1975). The focus is beyond the individual child, and the subjective feelings and judgements of others become of paramount importance (Smith et al. 1988; Wicks-Nelson and Israel 1984). The person who perceives the child's behaviour as inappropriate plays a key role in the decision making, since what is viewed as problem behaviour and how it is defined, interpreted and treated are 'as much as a function of the perceiver as they are of the behaver' (Graubard 1973: 246). Therefore, the locus of responsibility is placed upon, and raises many issues for, all professionals, that is, the teacher, psychologist, social worker or psychiatrist, since their attitudes, sensitivity, tolerance and ability to cope are bound to influence how children are perceived and handled (Wicks-Nelson and Israel 1984; Upton 1983).

The ecosystemic approach

In ecosystemic terms, children and their behaviour cannot mean-ingfully be seen in isolation from their context. Behaviour is seen as the result of the dynamic interrelationships and interactions between personal and environmental variables between and within different systems where the child finds him/herself, that is, family, early years setting, community etc (Vasta et al. 1992; Pellegrini 1987; Davie 1986; Bronfenbrenner 1979). The eco-systemic approach assumes that there is no linear cause and effect for a problem, but that behaviour is maintained by the total interaction and not just by reinforcement (Brown 1986). For example, a young child's behaviour may be the result of the inter-actions with other children or adults, or because of the layout of the room such as crowding conditions, few resources and equip-ment. The introduction of the ecosystemic approach was an impor-tant step in understanding the complexities of human behaviour, since instead of employing an inside–outside dichotomy, it empha-sised the study of interrelationships between and within systems which affect behaviour (Burden 1981; Prugh et al. 1975). The causes of any instance of problem behaviour are part of a complex formation of actions and reactions between the participants (Käser 1993; Molnar and Lindquist 1989; Burden 1981).

In line with these views, children's behaviour started to be understood as a function of its context (Kauffman 1988). In the school context, in particular, the root of behavioural difficulties started to be examined in terms of interactions in the classroom. Burden (1981: 35) argues that 'the explicit and implicit organisational structure of a school affects the perceptions and behaviour of its pupils in a way that leads them to be seen as problematical or disruptive by those faced with the task of maintaining that structure'. In the light of the interactionist/labelling and ecosystemic perspective, terms such as 'disturbing', 'disruptive' and 'challenging' behaviour have been introduced in the field of education.

Disturbing-disruptive and challenging behaviour

Algozzine (1980: 112) states that it is not simply the level and type of behaviour which a child exhibits that may result in his/her being identified as disturbed; it is the fact that 'particular sets of characteristics which make him/her an individual result in differential reactions . . . from others within the child's ecosystem'. In this context, the child's behaviour is seen more as 'disturbing' rather than 'disturbed'. According to Lawrence et al. (1984), the term 'disturbing' seems more promising since it does not attempt to prejudge the nature of problems experienced by the children and it does not rule out that these problems may have more to do with the experience the child confronts than with any inherent defect in the child her/himself. Similar arguments underpin the use of the term 'challenging' behaviour which implies adults' inability to respond appropriately.

Davie (1986) suggests that before any individual child's behaviour is considered as disturbing, professionals should (i) think whether the behaviour is a call for help or attention, (ii) consider possible inner conflicts or external events which may be responsible for or trigger such behaviour and (iii) critically examine whether their own attitudes, perceptions and classroom rules create the child's difficulties.

Concluding remarks

The terms and definitions discussed in this chapter have been developed mainly with adolescents and older children in mind; however, an understanding of the theories which have influenced the terms and definitions of behaviour problems may shed some light on the conceptualisation of behaviour problems in the early years. From the previous discussion it is evident that, over the years, a shift has been made from an inside–outside dichotomy regarding the aetiology and causes of behaviour problems to interactionist approaches and ecosystemic approaches which emphasise the impact of dynamic interactions within and between different systems and the way they affect behaviour.

It appears, however, that no single definition is satisfactory to all those professionals dealing with children. Wood (1982) suggests that any definition used to refer to children's behaviour problems should include certain elements, in order (i) to be of help in understanding the philosophical and organisational context and the goals of particular educational settings and (ii) to inform intervention planning for meeting children's needs. These elements refer to:

i.   what or who is perceived to be the focus of the problem (the 'disturber' element);
ii. how the problem behaviour is described (the 'problem behaviour' element);
iii. in which setting the problem behaviour occurs (the 'setting' element);
iv. who regards the behaviour as a problem (the 'disturbed' element);
v.   what definition is used and by whom to differentiate disturbing from non-disturbing behaviour (the 'operationalising' element);
vi. whether the definition which is used informs assessment, planning for intervention and programme evaluation (the 'utility' element).

Still, the definition and terms used for behaviour problems are largely informed and guided by professionals' own background, theoretical orientation and duties and responsibilities. Consequently, in multi-professional practice, it becomes of crucial importance that all those involved with the assessment of, and intervention for, behaviour problems in young children clarify their definitions and provide an operational definition that will be the basis for any subsequent work.

Activity 3

Working with a colleague you may like to:

i.   list the terms which you use to refer to children's problem behaviour;
ii. describe the meaning which you accord to these terms;
iii. examine whether there is consistency in the terminology and definitions which you use.

Chapter 4

Behaviour problems in early years settings

The discussion in the previous chapter shows the lack of consensus about terms and definitions used to refer to children's behaviour problems. However, in educational settings, according to Galloway *et al.* (1982: xii–xiii), 'Most teachers have a fairly well-defined idea of what constitutes disruptive behaviour . . . they can identify the disruptive pupils in their classes without much difficulty.' The issue is that different teachers have different ideas as to what constitutes problem behaviour and tend to identify different pupils. What is seen as disruptive or problem behaviour by one teacher may be welcomed by another one and for both the same behaviour may change its significance depending on the time or the day of the week (Lawrence *et al.* 1984; Galloway *et al.* 1982).

The identification of behaviour problems, according to Kauffman (1989: 130), 'is a matter of judgment, an arbitrary decision based on an explicit or implicit value system'. This assertion may justify Galloway *et al.*'s (1982: xv) claim that disruptive behaviour can be seen 'as any behaviour which appears problematic, inappropriate and disturbing to teachers'. Mortimore *et al.* (1983: 1), however, take a more positive view to define disruptive behaviour in schools as 'any act which interferes with the learning, development or happiness of a pupil or his/her peers, or with the teacher's attempts to foster those processes or feelings'. This definition highlights teachers' understanding of the goals of education for children as another dimension that seems to influence the definition of behaviour problems.

In this context, to paraphrase Lawrence *et al.* (1984: 17), behaviour problems in educational settings are 'behaviour out of place'; behaviour is not disruptive by itself, but it becomes disruptive at certain times and in certain places. Problem behaviour then, defined in terms of the interactionist/labelling theories, is the result of systematic ordering which, consequently, involves rejection of inappropriate behaviour.

Behaviour problems in early years settings

In the same way, as has been indicated in the case studies outlined in the introduction, early years practitioners' judgements about children's behaviour are hardly informed or guided by any specific definition of behaviour problems or theoretical models. Nor do they use any specific criteria to make judgements about the children's behaviour. As with teachers in schools, early years practitioners tend to understand and consider children's problem behaviour in the light of (i) their own understanding and expectations of children's behaviour at this particular age and (ii) the goals and expected outcomes pursued in the particular educational contexts.

Behaviours such as hyperactivity and aggression (shown in Rory's case) that might threaten the early years practitioners' ability to deal with them and the timing and the place where specific behaviours are exhibited (e.g. Tina's attention-seeking and Tony's 'clown' behaviour in a classroom context) are reasons for raising concerns about behaviour. Behaviours that are exaggerations of what is considered to be normal behaviour for particular ages (e.g. George's tension, Angelica's lack of friendships) and their persistence over a period of time (Tony's lack of adjustment) are also worrying signs.

Changes in behaviour after a period of satisfactory adjustment (as in James's case) and contradictory, puzzling and confusing behaviours (as in Tony's and Angelica's cases) are becoming the focus of attention and further investigation. Feelings, emotional state and well-being (e.g. being weepy, tense, withdrawn, lack of friendships etc) also represent an important dimension against which children's behaviours are perceived and identified as problematic. The continuous and dynamic process of social interaction that appears to shape and reshape certain behaviours (for instance, the way Tony's 'clown' behaviour was received and reacted to by other children with laughter and excitement, and the continuous presence of James's mother in the school vicinity) should receive early years practitioners' due attention.

A continuum of behaviours

Clearly, early years practitioners attend both to problem behaviours, such as acting out, disturbing and withdrawn behaviours, and children's positive behaviours and strengths. Galloway *et al.* (1982) observe that children's behaviour does not fall into two groups of normal or disruptive behaviours. Instead, it consists of a continuum from extremely cooperative to totally unacceptable and only a few children consistently remain at the same point on the continuum. Mortimore *et al.* (1983) agree with the subjective nature of judgements made about behaviour and state that many misbehaviours which fall within the bounds of 'normal' behaviour can nevertheless be very irritating for both teachers and those pupils who are trying to concentrate on work.

Again, considering the case studies in Chapter One, in most cases children's behaviour was not consistently placed within one or another dimension such as aggressive or withdrawn behaviours. It was rather a mixture of behaviours, identified either as positive, such as good social and language skills and perseverance, or negative, such as aggressive, hostile and withdrawn behaviours, that triggered the early years practitioners' concerns. Children's behaviour was placed on a continuum of behaviours ranging from extremely disturbing to positive and extremely withdrawn (Figure 4.1), indicating early years practitioners' concern for children's overall well-being.

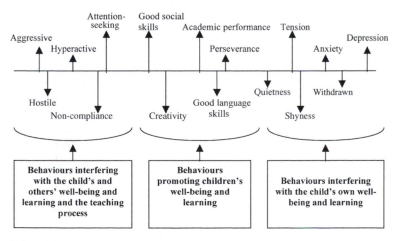

Figure 4.1 A continuum of behaviour in the early years.

Well-being and mental health in the early years

Consistent with early years practitioners' concerns, current policy also emphasises the promotion of children's well-being, as it enables them to fulfil their full potential and actively participate in everyday life. If children are exposed to experiences that make them feel good about themselves, then they enjoy positive relationships, learn confidently and overcome difficulties. In contrast, when they are overwhelmed with fears, anger, misery and pain, they experience all kinds of emotional and behavioural difficulties and problems (DfES 2001b).

Well-being is understood as a subjective state that is reflected in a range of feelings such as energy, confidence, openness, enjoyment, happiness, calm and caring which are combined and balanced (Stewart-Brown 2000). In young children, signs of well-being include self-confidence and self-esteem, openness, receptivity and flexibility, assertiveness and ability to defend oneself, vitality and enjoyment without constraints, relaxation and inner peace (Laevers *et al.* no date).

'Well-being' is also the main indicator of children's mental health. In general, mentally healthy children are expected to demonstrate the ability to play and learn, become aware of others and empathise with them, develop a sense of right and wrong, be able to face setbacks, resolve problems and learn from them, initiate and develop satisfying relationships and develop psychologically, emotionally, intellectually and spiritually. Those children who fail to meet these developmental milestones may be identified as having social, emotional and behavioural problems (DfES 2001b).

Both 'well-being' and 'mental health' are generic and broad terms that do not offer any specific criteria for identifying potential behaviour problems. However, they represent positive alternatives to terms that may have stigmatising connotations and signpost early years practitioners and teachers to aspects of behaviour and development that require attention. Children's failure to thrive in these aspects signals a need for further investigation and assessment in order to intervene early. Within this conceptual framework, the terms 'well-being' and 'mental health' are currently widely used in the early years.

A cognitive-affective model for understanding behaviour

Well-being and mental health can be better understood within a cognitive-affective framework. In the 1960s, the emphasis placed upon symptomatic behaviour started to be questioned and attention was shifted to the study of cognitive processes and their impact on behaviour. Social learning theorists and cognitive theorists started to study children's behaviour in terms of the ways they structure their experience and approach situations and, in particular, how they understand behaviour and imitate, modify and reproduce it (Harden *et al.* 2003; Ingram and Scott 1990; Levis 1990).

At the same time, the cognitive approach started to acknowledge the importance of emotions in explicit behaviour. Emotions were defined as states that are elicited by cognitive processing of external stimuli such as rewards and punishments, including changes in rewards and punishment, which, in turn, affect explicit behaviour (Rolls 1999). Carpenter and Apter (1988) argue that the way individuals perceive external stimuli affects the way they think and feel and, subsequently, the way they behave (Figure 4.2).

The cognitive approach, in acknowledging and embracing emotions, gave centrality to emotional development within educational contexts and, especially, in the early years when emotions account for and colour almost every experience of the young child. Its main influence on the management of behaviour problems has been the introduction of 'cognitive emotional' interventions which, according to Carpenter and Apter (1988), refer to a broad array of approaches that have emerged from developmental and social perspectives to deal with the emotional and behavioural difficulties exhibited by school-age children and youth.

In the 1990s, the notion of 'emotional intelligence' became influential in educational settings. The term is defined as 'the ability to perceive emotions, to access and generate emotions so as to

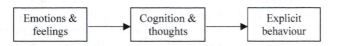

Figure 4.2 The relationship between feelings, cognition and explicit behaviour.

assist thought, to understand emotions and emotional knowledge, and to regulate emotion so as to promote emotional and intellectual growth' (Mayer and Salovey 1997: 5). The underlying concepts of emotional intelligence led to the development of the notion of 'emotional literacy' which has been introduced in educational settings to represent a framework for preventative approaches to problem behaviours (Weare and Gray 2003).

The conceptual framework of the cognitive-affective approach is of particular importance in the early years. Evidence from neuroscience suggests that in the early years the brain is remarkably plastic, shaping itself through repeated experience. Therefore, childhood is seen as offering 'a remarkable window of opportunity to give children the repeated experiences that will help them to develop healthy emotional habits – for self-awareness and self-regulation, for empathy and social skill' (Goleman 1997: xv). According to Shonkoff and Phillips (2000: 104), 'the young child's growing ability to regulate and integrate emotions adaptively into the fabric of social interactions . . . provides the foundations for psychological well-being and mental health'.

Classification systems for behaviour problems

Clinical classification systems

As there are many terms and definitions to refer to behaviour problems, there are also several systems of classifying them. These systems are divided into clinical and empirical. The most widely used clinical classification system is the 'Diagnostic Statistical Manual' (DSM) which has been developed 'to provide clear descriptions of diagnostic categories in order to enable clinicians and investigators to diagnose, communicate about, study, and treat the various mental disorders' (APA 1987: vii).

However, the DSM having been developed with adults in mind, it has been found unsatisfactory for use with children (Hallahan and Kauffman 1988). Achenbach and Edelbrock (1983) state that the dissatisfaction with DSM led the Group for the Advancement of Psychiatry (GAP) to develop the 'Psychopathological Disorders of Childhood' classification system which specifically provides child-oriented and theoretically-based classification of behaviour problems. GAP's classification system acknowledges the psychosomatic (that is, the interaction between mind and body), the psychosocial (that is, the child's interactions with family and society) and the developmental dimensions (that is, the need to look at the child in the context of stages of development) of problem behaviour (Gibbs 1982).

Still, GAP's classification system has been criticised as offering 'a mixture of narrative descriptions and theoretical inferences that provide no operational criteria for determining whether a child has a particular disorder' (Achenbach and Edelbrock 1983: 70). The consistent use of the GAP classification requires consistent understanding of the particular theory, which is not always the case. Even the most skilful professionals interpret and use the categories differently, mainly because of their particular understanding of different theories (Wicks-Nelson and Israel 1984).

Clinical classifications are of little use in educational settings. It is, however, necessary for educators to be familiar with the terminology of psychiatric classifications for making sense of and understanding psychological and psychiatric reports. The weaknesses and the inappropriateness of the psychiatric classification systems have led many clinicians and researchers to analyse empirical data collected through questionnaires and checklists (Kauffman 1989; Quay 1972).

Empirical classification systems

During the 1960s and 1970s, teachers' responses to different behaviour checklists were factor-analysed to identify behavioural dimensions that best reflected teachers' understanding of behaviour problems (Kauffman 1989; Bauer and Shea 1989; Wicks-Nelson and Israel 1984; Quay 1972). Such analyses revealed two broad behavioural dimensions labelled variously by different researchers (Table 4.1). The terms conduct problems, externalising problems, antisocial behaviour and over-acting behaviours imply a tendency to express impulses against others and society, while the terms personality problems, internalising problems, neurotic behaviours and under-acting behaviours contain a variety of elements suggesting low self-esteem and social withdrawal (Achenbach and McConaughy 1987; Harre and Lamb 1986; Kohn and Rosman 1973; Rutter 1965).

Quay (1972), reviewing a number of statistical studies, applied in diverse samples of children, found two more behavioural dimensions alongside the two broad dimensions, that is, immaturity

Table 4.1 Broad dimensions of behaviour problems revealed by empirical studies undertaken among teachers.

Studies	Broad dimensions of behaviour problems	
	Conduct problems	Personality problems
Petterson (1961) Achenbach and Edelbrock (1983)	Externalising problems	Internalising problems
Rutter (1965, 1967)	Antisocial behaviour	Neurotic behaviours
Stott *et al.* (1975)	Over-acting behaviours	Under-acting behaviours

and socialised delinquency. Immaturity is associated with young children and socialised delinquency with adolescents. Further factor analysis also revealed a number of behavioural sub-categories within each of the broad dimensions. Aggression, non-compliance, disruptive behaviours, inattention, hyperactivity and attention-seeking are behaviours identified within the broad dimension of conduct disorders. Anxiety, inferiority and withdrawal behaviours are classified under the personality disorders dimension and passivity and social immaturity are behaviours identified under the immaturity dimension (Bauer and Shea 1989).

Despite the diversity of instruments, subjects and statistical methods used, these broad and narrow dimensions of behaviour problems have been produced with considerable consistency across different studies (Achenbach and Edelbrock 1978). However, attention must be drawn to the fact that these dimensions may not be cross-culturally consistent. Often – especially in the early days – checklists used for early screening had not been constructed and standardised on the basis of cultural, ethnic and racial differences (O'Donnell and Cress 1975).

Dimensions of behaviour problems in the early years

Analyses of preschool teachers' ratings have also revealed two broad bipolar dimensions, that is, 'anger-defiance' and 'apathy-withdrawal', which are similar to those found in the general population of children and labelled as conduct problems and personality problems, respectively (Kohn and Rosman 1973). These bipolar

Figure 4.3 Dimensions of behaviour problems in the early years.

dimensions have been contrasted with positive aspects of behaviour such as cooperation and compliance for anger and defiance and interest-participation for apathy and withdrawal (Figure 4.3).

Some other studies have identified a third dimension which, although variously defined, reflects developmentally related problems (Table 4.2). This dimension includes destructiveness and hyperactivity (Rubin and Clark 1983; Behar and Stringfield 1974), immaturity and social isolation (St James-Roberts *et al.* 1994; McGuire and Richman 1986b), and developmentally related problems such as lack of motor control and clumsiness, communication problems, difficulties in cooperation, poor concentration and perseverance (Papatheodorou 1995). It is expected that, as children grow and absorb experiences, they will outgrow these developmentally related problems. Clark (1986: 5), however, points out that 'Early experience *per se* does not, unless reinforced, possess crucially formative long-term effects.' Indeed, research undertaken in early years settings has shown that it is the quality of early years experience that makes a difference and has a long-lasting effect on children's future development, behaviour, learning and life opportunities (Melhuish 1993; Sylva and Wiltshire 1993; Schweinhart *et al.* 1993).

Table 4.2 Broad dimensions of behaviour problems in the early years.

Preschool studies	Broad dimensions		
Behar and Stringfield (1974), Rubin and Clark (1983)	Hostile-Aggressive	Anxious-Fearful	Hyperactive-Distractible
McGuire and Richman (1986b), St James-Roberts *et al.* (1994)	Conduct, Restless, Aggressive behaviours	Emotional, Miserable behaviours	Social isolation, Immaturity
Papatheodorou (1995)	Conduct problems	Emotional problems	Developmentally related problems

Research in the neurobiological, behavioural and social sciences has clearly demonstrated the influence of the quality of early life experiences on (i) the development of brain and human behaviour, (ii) powerful and complex emotions and social skills developed during the early years, and (iii) early relationships which either support or constitute a risk for adaptation (Shonkoff and Phillips 2000). Arguably, developmental and maturational factors alone cannot be understood as compensating for children's behaviour difficulties and problems, in the long term.

The empirical classification system has gained credibility in education mainly because it allows children's behaviour to be examined in terms not only of quality but of quantity as well. Behaviour checklists allow identification of behaviours that may fall across all dimensions, but to varying degrees; they do not provide the discrete categories elicited by the clinical classification, but continuous dimensions along which a child's behaviour may be placed according to the number of problem behaviours s/he exhibits. In this way, a child may be identified as exhibiting multiple problems rather than placed in one category (Papatheodorou 1995; Kauffman 1989; Quay *et al.* 1987).

In general, the empirical classification system provides a more functional framework for teachers and early years practitioners to understand behaviour problems than the clinical system (Epstein *et al.* 1985). In practice, however, there is often cross reference to all different systems. It is important, however, to remember that, as the different classification systems have been developed differently and for different purposes, they may identify different behaviours at different rates and not always the same children (Tharinger *et al.* 1986). This comment raises, once again, the fundamental question of how behaviour problems are defined. Kauffman (1989: 130) observes that:

> behavior disorder is not an all-or-nothing phenomenon. How different an individual's behavior must be from that of others before we invoke the label disordered is a matter of judgement. . . . That judgement may be guided by statistical analyses, but the statistics themselves are not sufficient.

Rutter (1977) argues that any classification system must take into account, and fulfil, a number of criteria: it must

i.   be based on facts and not on concepts;
ii. be defined in operational terms which aim to classify problem behaviour and not children;
iii. convey information which is practicable in ordinary practice;
iv. provide adequate coverage so that all aspects of problem behaviour and disorders are included;
v.   show logical consistency based on a set of principles and precise rules.

Whatever the limitations, the classification systems have a role to play by providing professionals with information that helps them to understand the nature of problem behaviour, informs screening and assessment and consequent intervention as well as helping to facilitate communication between all those involved directly, and sometimes indirectly, with the education and care of children.

Concluding remarks

Often behaviour problems in educational settings are behaviours 'out of place'. Behaviours are considered problematic because of the timing and place where they occur. In young children, behaviour problems are often understood in terms of children's well-being and learning, and judgements about children's behaviour are implicitly and explicitly informed by early years practitioners' and teachers' own understanding and expectations of (i) children's behaviour at this particular age range and (ii) the goals and expected outcomes pursued in early years settings. Signs that raise concerns for potential threat to children's well-being and mental health and possibly the development of behaviour problems include exaggerations of, or deviations, from 'normal' or expected behaviours, sudden changes in behaviour, contradictory, inconsistent and puzzling behaviours, persistent inappropriate behaviours and behaviours that threaten or undermine practitioners' ability to deal with them.

There are two major classification systems of children's behaviour problems, that is, the clinical and empirical. The two systems have been developed differently and for different purposes. As such, they tend to identify different behaviours, at different rates and often different children. However, early years practitioners' awareness of these systems and their underlying philosophies is required because of their implications for the identification of, and intervention for, behaviour problems.

 Activity 4

In your setting, you may have children exhibiting problem behaviour. You may like to think about and list the early signs or behaviours which concerned you, explaining why.

Chapter 5

Factors associated with behaviour problems

A contextual framework

There are many factors that are associated with behaviour problems. Research findings have now shown that there is not one factor alone, but a dynamic interrelationship of many factors that account for the presence of behaviour problems in children. These factors will be examined at three different levels of functioning (see Figure 5.1) which reflect Bronfenbrenner's (1979) ecological theory, that is:

i. at micro level which represents the systems within which the child finds her/himself and whose functioning directly affect her/him, that is, the family and the early years setting;
ii. at meso level which represents the interactional process between and within systems and the way this interaction affects children's behaviour. The interaction between adults and children and family and early years setting will be considered here;
iii. at macro level which represents the broader community and existing services as well as societal values and attitudes.

Family factors

Often children's behaviour problems are explained and understood in terms of family circumstances and failings. Social class, family structure, rearing practices and stresses such as separation from parents or lack of stable environments have all been studied to indicate repeatedly that the kind of experiences which children have do matter (Schaffer 1998). For example, regarding young

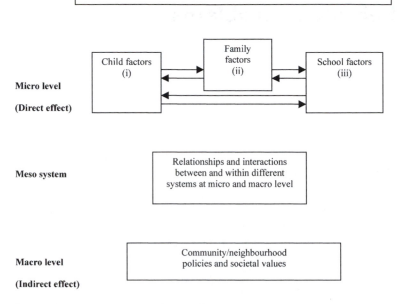

Figure 5.1 A representation of the dynamic interrelationship that affects children's behaviour.

i.   child's age, gender, academic performance, temperament;
ii. family's socio-economic background, values, rearing practices and quality of parenting, separation, single parenthood, secure and stable relationships, multiple and enduring adversity;
iii. school's/early years setting physical environment, class size, resources and play equipment, attendance period; early years practitioners'/teachers' interaction with children, labelling, stereotyping and self-fulfilling prophecy.

children, Golding and Rush (1986) have reported a strong relation between social class and the extent of exhibited temper tantrums, fighting, destructiveness and hyperactivity.

Davie *et al.* (1972) comment that these findings might be the result of the measures used to estimate the extent to which a child's behaviour in school deviates from 'normal' behaviour, with 'normal' behaviour being considered the kind of behaviour that is expected in educational settings which basically reflect middle-class values. There is therefore a need to acknowledge that, to a large extent, children's problems may be the result of the complex interrelationships and the conflicts arising because of different expectations and experiences and cultural mismatch between family and the school/early years setting environment (Weare 2000; Schaffer 1998; Gelfand *et al.* 1997).

Fergusson *et al.* (1990) claim that the major effect of social background on childhood is the influence of the non-observed vulnerability process, which, in turn, contributes to increased rates of childhood problems. Children's exposure to violence, fathers' aggression, mothers' psychiatric conditions, high rates of punishment and general marital discord and stressful home environment have all been found to be contributory factors, especially with conduct problems (Walker-Hall and Sylva 2001; Roff and Wirft 1984). It is suggested then that research and, of course, early years practitioners should move towards gaining greater understanding of how social conditions impact on the quality and nature of childhood rather than focus on social class which is an abstraction loaded with certain assumptions (Fergusson *et al.* 1990).

Single parenthood

Single parenthood has also been considered as a factor that adversely affects children. Again, it is essential to determine whether adverse effects occur as a result of the absence of a parent or whether they are linked to many financial and practical disadvantages that are often experienced by single-parent families. Research has shown that it is not single parenthood *per se* that affects children; rather, it is the many financial worries, poor and unacceptable accommodation and lack of choice about satisfactory arrangements for child care that, in turn, are likely to have an impact on children's mental health. Schaffer (1998: 89) points out that if single parenthood 'is not per se an at-risk factor then there is no reason to attach undue weight to it in decision making' and Ferri (1976), who has studied fathers' absence, points out that the belief that single parenthood is a detrimental factor to children's behaviour may be as harmful as any direct effects which the father's absence may actually have.

Child-rearing practices and quality of parenting

Children's psychological development has often been attributed to parenting styles and rearing practices (McFarlane *et al.* 1995; Davie *et al.* 1972). The relationships that young children establish with their parents are generally considered vital to their well-being. Low-quality parenting characterised by hostile, punitive, authoritarian, inconsistent behaviours and lack of warmth and affection has been repeatedly associated with children's psychological development and problems (Walker-Hall and Sylva 2001).

However, it is important to note here that children's psychological development and problems should not be explained entirely in terms of parenting, assuming a one-way process. The fact is that parenting is a bidirectional process where parents and children are influenced by and influence each other. Thomas and Chess (1977, 1984) have clearly demonstrated this with their seminal New York longitudinal study where they found that the child or parental characteristics alone are not good predictors of children's later behaviour. It is rather the fit or lack of fit of the characteristics of both the child and the parents that affects the interactional process.

Secure and stable relationships

Freud was the first to draw attention to the importance of children's early experiences and emotional bond with their mother in the formation of their personality. Later on, Bowlby (1979) also emphasised the importance of attachment – that is, a close and satisfying relationship with the mother during the formative years of childhood – for children's healthy personality development. In more recent years, there has been a growing appreciation and understanding of the relationships developed between members of the family. Any disruption of the relationships within the family because, for instance, of parental separation and/or divorce, or of illness, depression or death of a parent, has been considered as potentially detrimental to the child in the short and/or long term (Schaffer 1998).

Multiple and enduring adversity

It is now acknowledged that no single event or factor can explain behaviour. Schaffer (1998: 109) comments that 'it is the totality of a child's experiences that matters rather than single events. . . . Distorted family relationships are much more likely to be influential because they, after all, can exercise that influence throughout the whole of childhood instead of impinging only at one particular period.' The emphasis then is placed as far as possible on pre-serving continuity of relationships, environments and routines to make life predictable.

The educational and early years setting

There is a substantial body of research indicating that schools affect the behaviour of their pupils. Rutter and his colleagues, from their extensive work on this issue, have concluded that there are indica-tions that the schools may influence children's behaviour either positively or negatively (Rutter 1985; Rutter *et al.* 1974, 1979). However, the question often posed is whether the school affects the children or the children shape the functioning of the school. Testing this hypothesis, Rutter and his colleagues found that although pupils' characteristics shape their teachers' behaviour there is also an influence on children stemming from the character-istics of the school environment (Rutter 1985; Maughan *et al.* 1980). While most of this work has been conducted at secondary school level, the evidence nevertheless indicates that school factors can influence pupil behaviour as much as factors associated primarily with the child and the family (Galloway and Goodwin 1987).

The physical environment

The importance of the physical environment in facilitating children's learning and behaviour in educational settings has long been recognised by teachers, especially in early years settings and pri-mary schools where resources and equipment to stimulate the development of skills and the arrangement of the physical environ-ment to produce dedicated areas of interest are common features. Shonkoff and Phillips (2000) state that the 'well-being' and 'well-becoming' of young children are dependent, as much as on stable and loving relationships with adults, on safe and predict-able environments, within the educational settings and in the broader environment, that provide a range of growth-promoting experiences.

Jamieson *et al.* (2000), quoting Pouler, argue that the way the space is organised implies a certain order, determines what may happen and in a way locates and commands individuals. It has now been realised that uncomfortable and unmanageable environments are disruptive forces that leave pupils feeling neglected and alienated. On the other hand, physical environments that are planned to offer opportunities for shared activity, communication and cooperation and facilitate problem solving allow children to co-construct their knowledge of the world (Gandini 1998).

Classroom space, class size, play equipment and outdoors facilities

Classroom space seems to be associated with the level of children's motor activity, but the level of aggressive behaviour tends to remain unchanged irrespective of classroom size (Burgess and Fordyce 1989; Smith and Connolly 1980). Similarly, large classes are less enjoyable and more exhausting for staff, but there is not always a clear association with more behaviour problems in them (Baker et al. 1985; Smith and Connolly 1980). It seems that it is the crowding conditions (that is, the ratio between classroom space and number of children) and pupil–teacher ratio that make a difference rather than classroom space and class size, separately. Aggressive behaviour, in particular, is subject to crowding conditions which tend to have physiological, behavioural and social consequences which build up over time (Aiello et al. 1979; Loo 1972).

An environment with little play equipment is often reported as being stressful and leading to instrumental aggressive behaviour, that is, fights over equipment available (Smith and Connolly 1980), but the quality, appropriateness and suitability of resources for facilitating children's play activities and behaviour are more important factors determining the frequency of behaviour problems (Papatheodorou 1995). Indeed, regarding outdoor facilities, research has shown that it is the presence of very good equipment that makes a difference, especially, to developmentally related problem behaviours (Papatheodorou 1995). Young children tend to display significantly fewer developmentally related problems in nursery schools with very good outdoors facilities. Good playgrounds which offer different equipment, textures and colours can offer developmentally appropriate opportunities to children to stretch their bodies and emotions to new limits, develop dynamic balance, stimulate their senses, manipulate items, and begin to interact with others and learn problem solving (NPPS 2000).

Attendance period

Overall, children attending morning sessions tend to exhibit fewer behaviour problems than children attending afternoon sessions (Papatheodorou 1995; Davies and Brember 1991). It is suggested that both children and teachers may be more tired in the afternoon and this may cause deterioration in children's behaviour and the teachers' reaction to such behaviour. Parental choice of attendance session may also explain the differences between morning and afternoon sessions; Davies and Brember (1991) state that the more organised parents tend to use the morning sessions, whereas the less organised choose the afternoon sessions, and so assume that differences in problem behaviour between children attending morning and afternoon sessions may reflect different rearing practices and parental attitudes and values.

The early years curriculum

At a recent conference, McNamara (2003), in her keynote speech, among other variables identified curricular demands as being closely associated with children's behaviour problems. Among early years practitioners, there is also a concern that, within a culture and climate dominated by the values of academic achievement, children's social and emotional development may be overlooked. Early years practitioners and teachers may drift from the essence and importance of their work, which is children's holistic development, and shift their attention to skills that children need to acquire in order to succeed in forthcoming testing in such areas as language, mathematics and science. The lack of any requirement and the difficulties of defining a prescribed model for assessment of social and, especially, emotional and personal development (which is not readily observable) may further reinforce such attitudes. Within this climate of competing and often conflicting values and practices, inevitably, concerns have been expressed for children's behaviour by practitioners who need resources and strategies that will systematically support children's well-being and mental health (Shonkoff and Phillips 2000).

Early years practitioners' and teachers' training

Early years practitioners' and teachers' training has been found to be a factor that is associated with the identification of behaviour problems (that is, as acting out, withdrawn or developmentally related) in young children. In general, nursery teachers with longer training report more developmentally related problems, but this is not the case for conduct and emotional problems. Nursery teachers who identify their training as being balanced, in terms of theory and practice, are those who show greater awareness of all different types of behaviour problems. It is suggested that training is an important factor, but not so much in terms of its length as in the quality of the training received (Papatheodorou 1995).

Teaching experience is another factor that needs to be considered here. Nursery teachers new to the profession tend to identify more conduct problems, whereas their colleagues with long teaching experience tend to identify more emotional problems (Papatheodorou 1995). In general, the more experienced the teachers, the fewer the behaviour problems they perceive (Borg and Falzon 1990). These findings seem to reinforce the view that experience is a mediating factor that shapes adults' attitudes towards young children's problem behaviour (Veeman 1987).

The interaction between early years practitioners and children

One of the most important variables associated with children's behaviour is the early years practitioner and teacher him/herself. Research has shown that teachers are influenced by their perceptions of children's behaviour, which then affect their interaction with children and the way they treat them. Cooper (1989: 180) argues that 'the manner in which teachers and pupils relate to one another is of crucial significance in the matter of disruptive behaviour and pupil disaffection'. It is then important to understand the subtle processes that take place in the relationships and interactions established between children and the early years practitioners and teachers.

The initial perceptions and impressions which teachers form about the children are important as they may become the basis for categorising and even stereotyping them. Like anyone else, teachers selectively pay attention to particular items of information, while they ignore others. The information to which teachers attend is to a large extent determined by their own attitudes, values and personal and professional philosophies as well as temporary states of mood due to personal events and difficulties (Doney 1977). In addition, the type of the educational setting, its organisational and administrative arrangements and the demands made upon them together with the way in which the class is organised and managed also become important factors in the kind of children's attributes and other information to which the teachers attend (Rogers 1982). This information forms the basis on which children may be categorised according to dimensions that are important for teachers, that is, either academic achievement or behaviour. If behaviour is an important dimension for the teacher, and children's behaviours (and sometimes children themselves) are categorised either as 'good' or 'bad', then, if care is not exercised, children may be stereotyped accordingly (Leach 1977). Once children have been stereotyped in a particular way, it is often difficult for them to make a new or different impression upon their teachers. Some pupils may become 'locked in' to a particular set of characteristics that their teachers have assumed them to have (Rogers 1982).

Once pupils have been categorised into a particular type, teachers inevitably make some tentative predictions about their future behaviour and start to form certain expectations for them (Hargreaves 1972). Such expectations tend to guide teachers' responses and actions which, in turn, affect children's outcomes (Good and Brophy 1991). In the case of children's behaviour, if teachers' expectations are accurate and open to feedback, it is likely to lead them to behave in a way that sustains and reinforces children's behaviour (Good and Brophy 1991; Brophy 1985; Brophy and Good 1974).

In addition, teachers' expectations for their pupils' behaviour may come to serve as a self-fulfilling prophecy which is defined as 'an expectation or prediction, initially false, which initiates a series of events that cause the original expectation or prediction to become true' (Brophy and Good 1974: 35). Teachers, on the basis of their initial expectations, start to behave in ways that lead children to respond in such ways as to strengthen the initial expectations. Self-fulfilling prophecies emerge when perceivers such as early years practitioners and teachers act 'consistently' or 'in accordance' with their expectations (Miller and Turnbull 1986:

238). This has clearly been evident in Fry's (1983) study which has shown that children who exhibit problem behaviour receive more negative feedback and obtain fewer social contacts, with the result that their interaction with the teachers deteriorates. For these children their behaviours are largely determined by the teachers' daily negative interactions.

The effect of labelling

There are clear warnings about the use of labels in general and, in particular, labels (e.g. emotional behavioural difficulties, aggressive, withdrawn) which refer to children in terms of what they lack rather than what they already have (Leach 1977). Labels that carry negative connotations tend to be particularly influential since 'a negative piece of information . . . typically carries more weight than a positive piece' (Rogers 1982: 73). Negative cues can easily generalise into negative types and therefore maintain or even enhance behaviours which are assumed by these cues. Early years practitioners and teachers should then avoid categories and be suspicious of the organisational structures and policies which encourage, or seem to confirm, categorisation. Instead, they should be open to new information which may shed light on existing perceptions of certain behaviours.

Academic performance

Academic performance is a factor that has frequently been the focus of research studies without always revealing consistent or conclusive findings. Some studies reveal behaviour problems to be associated with good academic performance whereas others associate them with low or poor performance. Regarding young children, acting out behaviours have frequently been associated with good academic achievement, whereas withdrawn and developmentally related problems are associated with low achievement (Papatheodorou 1995; Morgan and Dunn 1988). At this particular age, at which children's academic achievement is mainly judged informally, acting out behaviours may be seen as signs of high ability leading to good academic achievement. With shy, withdrawn and anxious children, although by no means unsuccessful, their performance may not be seen as comparable with the performance of the lively, acting out and 'visible' children who often are viewed optimistically as bright children (Morgan and Dunn 1988: 10). Often, with shy and withdrawn children who try not to be exposed, there is a danger that their progress is overlooked and their abilities underestimated.

The finding regarding developmentally related problems may be better understood if they are seen as the cause rather than the result of poor academic achievement. The presence of such developmentally related problems as difficulties in cooperation and communication, lack of concentration and perseverance, negative behaviour, being over-protected and lack of motor control/clumsiness may affect teachers' judgement of children's overall performance, leading to assumptions of low ability and low expectations (Papatheodorou 1995).

Some researchers accept that educational difficulties are more frequently the cause than the result of problem behaviour, while others consider educational difficulties as being a behaviour problem as well as a learning problem (Davie et al. 1972). Although such explanations have obvious value, they imply unidirectional causality. It would seem more realistic to conceive the relationship between behaviour problems and educational difficulties as more complex than is implied in any of the above arguments (Upton 1983). The DfES, cited in Clark (2003), has seen the situation as a 'virtuous circle' where better behaviour contributes to better teaching and learning and vice versa, while Wicks-Nelson and Israel (1991: 189) comment that 'once initial causation gets underway a more complex causal chain might operate, with all factors influencing others'.

The interactions between the family and the early years setting

The relationships within the family and within school represent one level of interactions that affect children's behavioural outcomes. Partnership between the early years setting and the family is another level of interaction that has demonstrated long-term effects on children's outcomes (Schweinhart et al. 1993). However, the benefits of such partnership are not limited to children only. Parents and practitioners can also be at the receiving end. Draper and Duffy (2001: 149) point out that 'working with parents from diverse communities widens their views on families and family life. There is a wide range of equally valid childrearing practices and patterns of family life. Differences can be shared, respected and explored.'

The importance of the interaction between these two systems has been clearly worded in governmental policies which point out that 'a strong relationship with parents encourages continuity for the child, good communication, participation and ownership' (HSMO 2003; DfES 2002).

The broader community

Rutter and and Garmezy (1983: 834) argue that 'the social status of the area may be as (or more) important than the social status of the individual'. Indeed, Randall (1991) observes that the incidence of aggressive behaviour among infants ranges from 5 to 20 per cent depending largely on the catchment area of the school. Schools in areas with a poorer socio-economic background tend to have more incidences of aggressive behaviours and early years teachers tend to identify more behaviour problems in deprived than affluent areas (Papatheodorou 1995).

It is argued that children who live in deprived and densely populated urban areas, whose parents have low levels of education or low income, are those who are socially and culturally deprived. Socio-economic deprivation leads to low educational levels within the family and subsequently in the broader environment of the community (Alimisi 1988; Eliou 1978). Children living in areas of socio-economic deprivation are more likely to be susceptible to, and defeated by, the invisible mechanisms which perpetuate the social class structure and operate as an obstacle to educational success (Tzani 1986).

Upton (1983) states that it is not clear whether the reported rates of behaviour problems reflect real area differences or differences in detection and reporting procedures. It is suggested that the socio-economic status of the area may affect the availability of support services, both statutory (e.g. social services, health services, school psychological services) and voluntary, and non-governmental services (like advice and support groups) and the quality of the schools (Nikolopoulou and Oakland 1990). It is likely that, in areas with good services, more children will be identified and offered support than in areas with limited and inadequate services.

Also, community norms and attitudes, temperamental and child-rearing differences between different regions and locations may influence the rate of the identified problems (Langfeldt 1992; Davie *et al.* 1972). Cultural differences between different areas may also represent some of the factors which maintain and reproduce differences in pupils' outcomes, although the underlying mechanisms are complex and not yet clearly defined. The expansion of preschool provision, at least in western societies, highlights particular societal attitudes towards the care and education of young children. At the same time, governmental initiatives such as Head Start and Sure Start, which aim to support young children who are 'at risk' and their families, reflect current societal attitudes and values towards childhood in general, and children's experiences in particular. Such attitudes and values, expressed through policies, are expected to affect the way children are treated and their needs are met.

Concluding remarks

Research evidence has shown that behaviour and, consequently, problem behaviours are the result of complex and dynamic interrelationships between personal and environmental factors, both social and physical. Early years practitioners may have little, or limited, control of some of these aspects of children's lives, but it is important that they consider and are sensitive to the implications of such factors for their decisions.

 Activity 5

Consider any child whose behaviour raises concerns in your setting and think about the factors which may contribute to the child's behaviour.

i. Are there any factors which you think are more important than others?
ii. Do you have enough information to make any judgements about these factors?

Part II

Support for positive behaviour

Chapter 6

Behaviour management (i)

Habitual preventative strategies

Behaviour management

Shea (1978: 263) has defined behaviour management as 'all those actions (and conscious inactions) which educators take in order to assist children to develop effective behaviours that are personally self-fulfilling, productive, and socially acceptable'. Such actions include a broad range of activities, such as arranging the learning environment, establishing and maintaining classroom rules and procedures, providing guidance, instructions and rationales and dealing with occurring misbehaviour (Martin and Norwich 1991). Behaviour management is associated with safe, caring and productive environments where children are respected as intelligent persons (Cooper and Upton 1992).

Roberts (1983), however, argues that even positive behaviour management would be unacceptable if confining or inhibiting behaviour were either the intention or the outcome. But although systems of suppression and distortion of children's personal development must be ruled out, it is argued that systems of facilitating children's behaviour and learning should be adopted (Kerr and Nelson 1989; Roberts 1983). Early years practitioners and teachers consistently endorse and manifest beliefs about child-centred practice where they view themselves as facilitators (Kagan and Smith 1988), that is, 'in responding, rather than initiating, in following the child's lead and elaborating on what the child expresses an interest in' (Mowder and Widerstrom 1986: 172). They also claim that in environments where children are engaged in age-appropriate activities of their own choice, problem behaviours are not an issue. However, this situation appears to be rather an idealistic description of early years settings. As has already been discussed in previous chapters, young children often exhibit problem behaviours and early years practitioners experience concerns about the management of these behaviours. In addition, early years practitioners and teachers operate 'in loco parentis' and the way they manage or fail to manage children may affect children's sense of autonomy and self-discipline (Denscombe 1985; Roberts 1983).

Therefore, approaches, strategies and techniques which they adopt are crucial in preventing, and/or managing, problem behaviours. According to Roberts (1983). there are two styles of classroom behaviour management, that is, (i) the habitual style which helps teachers and early years practitioners to establish a normal atmosphere in the classroom and (ii) specific techniques which are employed to deal with specific incidents of behaviour problems that occur. The first style is preventative in nature and aims to reduce problem behaviours which require the employment of specific techniques (Kerr and Nelson 1989).

Habitual preventative behaviour management

Research has now shown that the quality of early years experience has a long-lasting determining effect on children's future development, behaviour, achievement and life opportunities (Melhuish 1993; Sylva and Wiltshire 1993; Schweinhart et al. 1993). However, early experiences may not have a formative long-term effect unless they are carefully planned, reinforced, monitored and evaluated on the basis of existing knowledge about children's behaviour, in general, and problem behaviour, in particular.

Habitual behaviour management techniques aim systematically to facilitate and support children's well-being demonstrated in their ability for self-regulation, cooperation, perseverance, resolution of conflict, expression of feelings and capacity for empathy, compassion and love (Porter 2003; Shonkoff and Phillips 2000; Bronson 2000). Considering the contextual nature of many problem behaviours, (discussed in Chapter Five), habitual behaviour management techniques are planned in order to address (i) environmental factors and curricula issues, (ii) the interactions and relationships created between adults and children, and between early years setting and family, and (iii) any misbehaviour occurring.

The environment of the early years setting

There is now growing evidence that environmental conditions, both physical and social, have great impact on current and future prospects for children's social problems (Bronson 2000). Malaguzzi argues that the environment becomes part of the individual so that 'any response to a request we make of the children or to a request that children make of adults is facilitated or obstructed by the environment and its characteristics' (cited in Gandini 1998: 166). This view is supported by Greenman who claims that the environment conditions how one feels, thinks and behaves; it either works for the individual or against him/her (cited in Gandini 1998) by either stimulating or restricting children's experiences (Rodger and Ziviani 1999). In line with these arguments and in order to facilitate and promote children's well-being (Shonkoff and Phillips 2001; Gandini 1998), it is important to create an 'emotionally safe environment' (Figure 6.1), where children feel that they can do things and their doings are acknowledged, leading to a sense of pride (Lourens 2004). They are allowed to be in touch and express their feelings, they are offered opportunities to think and solve problems, make choices, be responsible and, ultimately, feel that they are loved and belong. According to Malone and Langone

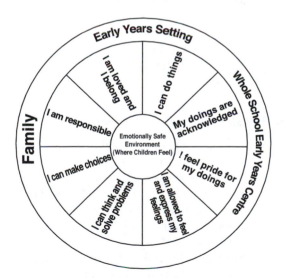

Figure 6.1 An emotionally safe environment.

(1999), environmental arrangements represent the first and the least directed and intrusive form of intervention.

The physical environment

In early childhood programmes, according to Hanline (1999), the physical environment provides the foundation for a play-based curriculum that promotes engagement in appropriate behaviours and interaction. Research undertaken among primary school children has shown that pupils value places which allow active and energetic play as well as places which offer tranquillity and fun. Aesthetically decorated, clean, tidy and noise-free places are part of children's requirements as they are places which facilitate cooperative play, investigation and problem-solving learning. Playfulness and imagination are the striking elements of children's preferable environments, as are hygiene and safety (Papatheodorou 2002b). In general, the physical environment (both indoors and outdoors) should be organised in a way that offers opportunities for children to experience autonomy, exercise choice, communicate and interact with others. In general, early years settings or classrooms which have been organised to actively engage children in play activities are less likely to present problem behaviours (Porter 2003; Bronson 2000; Iacono 1999). However, providing an environment that does not present any challenges may not always serve children the best way. Children also need an environment which offers opportunities for risk taking as well as experiencing failure within a supportive context that matches and extends their skills (Rodger and Ziviani 1999).

Class space and size, and adult–child ratio

The research findings are not conclusive with regard to the association of behaviour problems and class space and size; however, the evidence is that (i) in large spaces there are higher levels of motor activity, energetic play and noise, (ii) crowding conditions cause discomfort and aggressive tendencies and (iii) teaching in larger classes is more tiresome and less enjoyable for teachers and early years practitioners (Burgess and Fordyce 1989; Baker *et al.* 1985; Smith and Connolly 1980). These observations, together with children's need to have quiet, relaxing and calming areas (Papatheodorou 2002b; Hanline 1999), signify the importance which needs to be placed on classroom space and size. A well designed play space should take into account spatial density and size, and spatial arrangements should clearly define boundaries to allow for solitary and quiet activities as well as to encourage group activities and social interaction (Rodger and Ziviani 1999).

With regard to adult–child ratio, although this is legally controlled, it should still be determined so that all children have appropriate individual attention without being overshadowed (Porter 2003). Too much adult supervision may be as detrimental to children's autonomy, independence and initiative as too little supervision, which does not allow for individual children's needs to be met.

Routines, rites and rituals

Providing an age-appropriate routine which allows children to know what to expect and do throughout the day provides comfort and a sense of control over the environment (Porter 2003; Rogers 2002; Webster-Stratton 1999). Young children like stable and predictable environments which provide coherent and meaningful experiences for them (Bronson 2000). Systematic and programmed routines form the rites and rituals of an organisation showing its members 'what is expected from them' and 'how we do things here' (Kiley and Jensen 2003: 80). However, children also welcome surprising and unexpected events which are brief, fun and sensitively introduced so as not to upset the setting and its environment to the degree that they create feelings of insecurity and anxiety. Iacono (1999: 408–9) claims that 'embedding a novel aspect within familiar routine encourages the child to attend to the new information, thereby enhancing learning'.

Managing transitions

As children's sense of time is different from that of adults, information appropriate for young children's understanding of the daily routine is necessary. Visual or auditory cues are particularly useful to remind children about what they have to expect for the day or to make transitions from one activity to the next (Rogers 2002; Webster-Stratton 1999). For instance, having the daily programme in a sequence of photos means that children can see that story time follows after break time, or hearing a particular tune the children know that it is time to get ready for the next activity.

Clarity of expectations and guidelines

The establishment of guidelines for appropriate and expected behaviour from staff and children are helpful. Porter (2003: 23) states that guidelines are 'reference points' which make responses predictable across time and different situations, but they allow the early years practitioner or teacher to decide about his/her response depending on the circumstances. In general, rules with predetermined consequences should be avoided. Rogers (2002) points out that rules as well as expectations about communication, making requests and asking questions should be discussed and negotiated with the children.

Instructions, guidance and rationales

Whereas the organisation of the physical environment, the set-up of activities and the provision of resources aim to empower children to become autonomous problem solvers and resilient learners, sometimes early years practitioners need to provide direct instructions and guidance to address specific skills, or encourage prosocial dispositions which children need in order to be able to accomplish certain tasks and display appropriate behaviours (Spence 2003). For instance, the development of language and communication skills through instructions and guidance may help children to express their wishes, use conversational and social conventions, negotiate and take turns, with the result of preventing problem behaviours which occur because of the lack of these developmental skills (Porter 2003; Bronson 2000).

Discussions, guidance and rationales emphasise rationality by explaining why such behaviours are important, making explicit to children the consequences of their behaviour and allowing them to take responsibility for their actions, so contributing to the development of a sense of self-control (Bronson 2000). Explaining to a young child that 'pulling George's hair hurts him' is a better way of addressing a situation than reminding him/her that 'we keep hands and arms to ourselves'. In the same way, providing rational explanations to children may alter their irrational beliefs (Porter

2003). Explaining to a child that it is not the 'naughty' table which hurt her/him, but the fact that s/he fell over it because s/he was running provides rational explanations about children's experiences. Such explanations can be followed by a reminder of the expected behaviour in the setting.

Acknowledgement, praise and feedback

Acknowledgement of children's doings without making judgements and comparisons is one of the most powerful ways of enhancing children's self-esteem without attempting to manipulate them (Porter 2003). It offers children the opportunity to talk about their doings and achievements. Asking children individually whether they would like to talk about their work or explain why they have done things the way they did shows appreciation of the intrinsic value of their work rather than imposing adults' preconceived ideas about valuable activities.

Praise can be seen as a subtle way of manipulating children's behaviour (Porter 2003); however, it is not without value, especially when it is followed by descriptive feedback that brings about a sense of pride for the child. General praise words such as 'well done', 'good work' are too vague for the child. Instead, a 'well done' followed by a statement such as 'you have helped Ann to finish her work' gives clear and concrete messages and helps the child to attribute motives to her/himself and reinforces a sense of pride (Bronson 2000).

Relationships and interactions with children

The quality of interactions established between adults and children and among children is fundamental in supporting children's emotional and social needs (Porter 2003). Warm relationship, acceptance and appreciation, genuineness, empathy and affection can establish positive and fulfilling interactions (Lawrence 1996). Accepting and appreciating children's background, culture, abilities and competencies, and being non-judgemental and open to receive and examine any new information, eliminates the danger of forming rigid expectations that, if false, may have a detrimental expectancy effect on individual children.

Therefore, early years practitioners should get to know all children individually, try to understand their behaviour and show empathy for their actions. Empathy means sensing accurately the feelings behind the child's words and, in turn, communicating this back understanding (Milner and Carolin 1999; Lawrence 1996). Iacono (1999) states that responsive interactions, which take place within relaxed conversational exchanges rather than didactic sessions, offer the opportunity for early years practitioners to extend children's experiences on specific topics, facilitate turn-taking and express their own feelings and views. Using warmth and humour is often the best way to approach uncertain situations without causing embarrassment or humiliation for the child, while self-humour and introducing laughter can make learning fun and joyful (Rogers 2002). In such responsive interactions the child can be reassured that dislike for a particular behaviour does not reflect dislike for the child (Ahmad and Bano 1996; Fontana 1985).

Dealing with misbehaviour

Even in the best organised environment misbehaviours do occur and early years practitioners and teachers need to address them immediately and systematically and in a consistent manner. The way early years practitioners choose to do something, or not, has direct impact on either preventing, minimising or escalating behaviour. Tactical ignoring is one way of dealing with misbehaviour. Tactical ignoring is 'a conscious decision' not to attend to some problem behaviours which conveys non-verbal messages to all children (Rogers 2002: 66). It usually works with attention-seeking behaviours most common among young children. It is important, however, not to ignore behaviours that directly affect the child's and other children's well-being and learning. Non-verbal cues such as eye contact, staring, making certain gestures and moving physically towards or standing near the child are particularly effective with young children (Rogers 2002).

With young children, provision of additional materials, equipment and resources or restructuring the programme are also effective ways of minimising problem behaviours. The removal of objects that may attract children's attention or distract them from their task often helps them to concentrate on required tasks and demonstrate positive behaviours. Giving encouragement, guidance, affection and praise can help children to cope with anxiety, and the removal of the child from an activity when s/he becomes upset, frustrated or over-excited gives her/him time to relax or calm down. In some instances physical restraint may be used to prevent children from harming themselves or others. Physical restraint is risky and it is not recommended except as a last resort (Webster-Stratton 1999); staff should be aware of the guidance available regarding the use of restrictive physical interventions (DfES and DoH 2002). To deal effectively with misbehaviour these techniques should be systematically and consistently applied by all members of staff and parents, when appropriate, and soon after the misbehaviour occurs (Rogers 2002; Webster-Stratton 1999; Presland 1989; Nelson and Rutherford 1988).

Supporting and being supported by colleagues and parents

The organisation of, and practices established in, the early years setting aim to provide an emotionally safe learning environment which contributes to the prevention of problem behaviours. To achieve this, collaboration and communication between all members of staff involved and the parents themselves is required. Early years practitioners need to share the values underpinning practice and be consistent in their responses and dealings with children. Time for planning and reflection as well as for training should be available to establish practices that are based on good knowledge and strong evidence (Porter 2003).

There is now convincing evidence that communication and collaboration with parents has a long-lasting effect on children's outcomes (Schweinhart *et al.* 1993). Understanding children's cultural background, socio-economic conditions and specific family circumstances can help early years practitioners and teachers to offer support that meets children's emotional and behavioural needs (Webster-Stratton 1999). In addition, regular communication and information to, and from, parents will allow a shared understanding of what is best for individual children.

Concluding remarks

Behaviour management refers to all actions which early years practitioners and teachers need to take in order to prevent and/or deal with problem behaviours. It has positive connotations and rules out negative and authoritarian ideas of control and discipline. Habitual behaviour management refers to a wide range of strategies which aim to help children to develop skills for coping more effectively with problem-arousing situations, and adapt to stressful circumstances that are out of their control. They enable children to develop self-control of their actions rather being controlled by others through the imposition of strict rules. Habitual behaviour management supports children's well-being and prevents problem behaviours.

Activity 6

You may like to review and reflect together with other colleagues the current practice in your early years setting to:

i.   identify existing good practice;
ii. list areas which need further improvement and state how this might be achieved.

Chapter 7

Behaviour management (ii)

Approaches and strategies for early intervention

Historically the psychological models which influenced the definition and conceptualisation of behaviour problems have also influenced behaviour intervention approaches and techniques (Walker and Shea 1988). Most of the approaches have initially been developed by professionals working in different disciplines (mental health, clinical psychology); however, a number of them have been adopted and adjusted to be used in educational settings (Davies *et al.* 2004; Elliot and Place 1998; Mayhew 1997).

It is important that early years practitioners and teachers have an understanding of the underlying principles of different behaviour management approaches and techniques so as to be able to make informed decisions on the approach(es) and techniques they may use as well as when and under which circumstances to apply them in order to deal with identified problem behaviours (Kerr and Nelson 1989; Shea and Bauer 1987). In line with the different theoretical models discussed in Chapters Three and Four to explore terms for and definitions of behaviour problems, in this chapter the psychoeducational, behavioural, cognitive and ecosystemic approaches will be discussed and some techniques within each approach will be outlined.

The psychoeducational approach

The psychoeducational approach, consistent with the underlying concepts of the psychoanalytic theories, tends to address children's unconscious impulses and internal conflicts which are seen as the underlying causes of problem behaviours. According to the psychoeducational approach, early years practitioners' and teachers' major goal is to understand why children are behaving as they do and to establish a positive, trusting and meaningful relationship. The psychoeducational approach, according to Professor Weiss (2003), has a problem-solving orientation. Preventative behaviour management such as accepting children as they are, developing a mentally healthy classroom atmosphere, providing order and routine in the classroom schedule, and eliminating external stimuli causing disturbance is at the heart of the psychoeducational approach. However, a number of specific techniques (developed mainly by professionals from health and psychology) such as counselling, expressive arts and play have been found applicable in educational settings (Walker and Shea 1988; Shea and Bauer 1987).

Counselling

Counselling is defined as the process of listening to problems, advising on actions and explaining the constraints within which children should operate (Elliot and Place 1998). It aims to enable children to increase their conscious awareness of distorted perceptions of existing realities, and to provide emotional support in order to reduce their level of frustration (Davie 1989; Carpenter and Apter 1988). In general, counselling is seen as the process by which the child should be assisted to behave in a more rewarding manner.

There are two major styles of counselling: (i) the prescriptive or directive style, where the counsellor advises or guides the person undergoing counselling, and (ii) the facilitative or developmental style, where the counsellor is non-directive and seeks to encourage and support the individual in resolving his or her own problems and attaining rewarding experience (Murgatroyd 1985). Counselling is often viewed as highly skilled, requiring competence and substantial professional training. However, a great deal of counselling is practised by teachers who, as part of their role and responsibilities, often guide and instruct children (directive counselling) or facilitate them (facilitative counselling) to develop more appropriate and rewarding behaviours. Although limited, empirical support indicates that counselling in educational contexts can become highly effective, especially when it is used in parallel with behavioural techniques (Lavoritano and Segal 1992; Carpenter and Apter 1988).

The use of 'everyday life events' (Garfat 2002) and the 'life-space interview' (Redl 1971) are two approaches to counselling that are particularly useful with children. Both approaches take advantage of the little and seemingly unimportant events which happen in the child's everyday space, immediately after they occur, and involve for the counsellor to (i) provide immediate emotional support and (ii) take the opportunity to explore with the child both current and past experiences that affect her/his behaviour in order to plan for long-term support (Ward 2002). Successful application of both the 'everyday life events' and the 'life-space interview' approaches depends on (i) having clear ideas about the purpose and goals of the interview, (ii) taking into consideration the specific context in which behaviour occurs, (iii) considering the child's personal characteristics, (iv) having knowledge about child development and how to use it, (v) understanding the process of meaning-making, (vi) self-awareness and the ability to develop trustworthy relationships, (vii) having a framework for planning intervention and (viii) being an experienced interviewer (Garfat 2002; Shea and Bauer 1987). To make better use of the everyday events approach staff need to be observant and have good listening and communications skills, in order to understand children's thinking processes (Geldard and Geldard 1997). Such understanding will, consequently, inform long-term support rather than resulting in mechanistic responses (Ward 2002). Otherwise, there is the danger, as Elliot and Place (1998: 11) point out, that counselling will be 'misguidedly used as a euphemism for controlling behaviour'.

Finally, effective communication is an important variable that determines the course of counselling; paying attention to non-verbal behaviour, developing good listening skills, establishing trust, maintaining positive attitudes, developing expectations and showing non-judgemental attitudes and respect for privacy are basic skills required for counselling (Lawrence 1996).

Expressive arts and play

'Expressive arts' refers to interventions that encourage and permit children to express personal feelings and emotions in creative activities with minimal constraints (Walker and Shea 1988). Such techniques are more appropriate with young children, who are generally less capable of verbal communication and less in control of their personal life-events. Expressive arts, applied in an appropriate environment and under competent guidance, give children the opportunity to express their feelings and emotions and to reduce stress and frustration without the danger of conflict with others. Expressive arts include creative movement and dance, music, art therapy and drama, storytelling, free-play and role play.

Play in young children's development and learning has been highlighted and supported by many theorists and researchers and has influenced practice over the last few decades (Arthur *et al.* 1999; Tan-Niam 1994). Malone (1999: 307) argues that 'It is through play that children learn skills that they have not previously experienced, master newly acquired skills, [and] adapt those skills that have been learned and mastered.' He adds that 'problem-solving, planning, conflict and negotiation, personal/social boundaries, and the release of tension, frustration and aggression' (Malone 1999: 308) are some of the developmental and educational outcomes associated with play. Play is also considered essential to children's healthy development by offering concrete means of expressing their inner world. 'A major function of play is the changing of what may be unmanageable in reality to manageable situations through symbolic representation, which provides children with opportunities for learning to cope by engaging in self-directed exploration' (Landreth 2002: 12).

Expressive arts and play have been developed and used mainly by therapists in therapeutic settings by applying specific knowledge and skills. However, expressive arts constitute an important component of early years curricula and play is the vehicle for implementing the early years curricula. Malone and Langone (1999: 327), reviewing a number of studies, conclude that adults can assume a range of roles in children's play, such as 'the stage manager, mediator, co-players, scribe/observer, planner, director/ instructor, and leader'. Each of these roles requires a different level of involvement and intrusion in, and direction of, children's activities. These roles can be assigned in a continuum which ranges from the least intrusive/directive to the most intrusive/directive. Organizing the environment for play or taking the role of 'stage manager' involves the least intrusion and direction of children's play, whereas becoming a 'co-player' or 'instructor' involves gradually more intrusion and direction. As a co-player, the early years practitioner may indirectly guide children to a particular course of action and behaviour, and as an instructor may directly guide children on planned action.

Successful utilisation of expressive arts and play depends on adults' understanding and competencies in using them. The usage of expressive arts and play requires sensitive responses which are informed by the principles and ethos borrowed from therapy. Early years practitioners should (i) accept children as they are, not as they should be, (ii) develop a warm and friendly relationship and establish good rapport, (iii) establish a feeling of permissiveness so that children feel free to express their feelings, (iv) communicate the feelings back to children and allow them to gain an insight into their behaviour, (v) provide opportunities for children to solve their problems themselves and not to be manipulated or directed, (vi) plan the intervention process at individual children's pace and not be hurried and (vii) establish essential limitations to keep children safe and within the world of reality (Landreth 2002; Axline 1989).

The psychoeducational approach is based on the assumption that the problem resides within the individual and as such includes techniques that focus on the individual child. Expressive arts and play address children's inner world by encouraging them and giving them opportunities to express negative feeling indirectly and in an acceptable manner, whereas counselling goes a step further to allow children to talk through their difficulties and help them to develop socially acceptable behaviours.

The behavioural approach

The behavioural approach focuses on observable behaviour rather than on any underlying disorder within the individual or the individual's feelings and thinking (Porter 2000; Davie 1989; Nelson and Rutherford 1988). Its central thesis is that behaviour is acquired and maintained through learning explained in terms of reinforcement received from the environment (McBurnett et al. 1989). Behaviour is then studied in the context of the immediate environment and emphasis is placed on assessing current situational determinants of the behaviour, that is, what has preceded and followed certain behaviours (Levis 1990; McBurnett et al. 1989). Therefore, it is mainly the consequences or the possible consequences of the behaviour which actually control and reinforce the behaviour (Shea and Bauer 1987). Such consequences are known as reinforcers and constitute the main principle of the behavioural approach (Porter 2000; Milan 1990).

Shea and Bauer (1987) argue that a behavioural approach is only as effective as its reinforcers. The effectiveness of reinforcers is strongly determined by the extent to which they meet children's own needs. These needs may be made explicit by carefully observing or asking children about things they would like to have or do (Kazdin 1990; Presland 1989). Therefore, the identification and selection of appropriate reinforcers becomes of high significance in planning a behavioural intervention programme. Reinforcers are basically classified as (i) tangible or primary reinforcers (e.g. food, drinks, tokens) and (ii) social or secondary reinforcers (e.g. signs of approval, praise, smiles). These categories of reinforcers also reflect the developmental nature of children's preference for rewards. Primitive and concrete reinforcers such as edible and tangible ones are mainly applied to younger children, while the more abstract social reinforcers are often more appropriate for older children (Fantuzzo and Atkins 1992).

Behaviour change

On the basis of these underlying concepts, behaviourally oriented professionals have devised and implemented numerous intervention programmes, strategies and specific techniques which are classified into two major categories for behaviour change, that is, (i) behaviour enhancement procedures and (ii) behaviour reduction procedures (Kazdin 1990; Nelson and Rutherford 1988). In the behaviour enhancement procedures, rewarding techniques attempt to strengthen, maintain or increase the frequency of appropriate behaviour. In the behaviour reduction procedures, punishing techniques are used to eliminate the frequency of inappropriate behaviour.

A behavioural intervention programme involves a number of stages that need to be carefully planned. First of all, the problem behaviour is defined, recorded and measured. Then, the antecedents and consequences of the problem behaviour are determined (circumstances and events occurring immediately before and after the behaviour exhibited are recorded) and appropriate reinforcers are chosen. In the next stage, usually with the child's and parents' agreement, the programme is planned and implemented. Finally, the programme is systematically monitored and evaluated to decide the extent of changes in behaviour and whether the programme should be continued, altered or phased out (Kazdin 1990; Presland 1989; Shea and Bauer 1987; Merrett 1981).

Both behaviour enhancement and behaviour reduction have been found applicable in the classroom and across all age groups and all kinds of behaviour problems (Wheldall and Merrett 1992; Atwater and Morris 1988; Nelson and Rutherford 1988). In general in educational settings, teachers and early years practitioners prefer and use techniques which support appropriate behaviour (Trovato et al. 1992). Social reinforcement in the form of approval and praise has been found to be the most widely used and most effective technique, followed by token reinforcers. But the use of praise and token reinforcers in conjunction seems to further reinforce appropriate behaviour (Cameron and Pierce 1994).

Some researchers have reported mild punitive techniques to be effective, but generally punishment is considered as the least effective intervention. It results in the suppression of the undesirable behaviour at the time rather than in eliminating it in the long term (Levis 1990). It may teach children what not to do, but it does not provide any instruction in what they should do under the circumstances (Kaplan 1988). In particular, for young children, who often do not know what to do or how something must be done, punishment for mistakes may make things worse by bringing about anxiety and fear (Meayhew 1997; Kazdin 1990).

In terms of the behavioural approach, early years practitioners and teachers themselves constitute an important variable in dealing with behaviour problems. Many of the behaviours which teachers find disruptive are actually within their control. Teachers can modify and control pupils' behaviour by controlling their own responses (Thomas et al. 1968). The behavioural approach becomes effective only if teachers apply these techniques consistently, otherwise they may become confusing for both the child and the teacher.

Indeed, it is not always easy for teachers who deal with large classes to be consistent in applying these techniques with individual children. In many cases techniques appear to be time-consuming and interfere with the teaching process. The behavioural approach also raises ethical issues as it involves manipulation of children's behaviour without their consent and often against their will (Fontana 1985). As such, the behavioural approach becomes a means of controlling problem behaviour rather than facilitating positive behaviour. In addition, the behavioural approach has failed to demonstrate the maintenance, generalisation and transferability of behaviours over time and across different settings and situations (Porter 2000). Although the behavioural approach dominated the educational scene for almost two decades, it always remained controversial and teachers have been reluctant to fully embrace it (Nelson and Rutherford 1988; Docking 1980).

The cognitive-affective approach

The cognitive-affective approach has been particularly influential in behaviour management. The acknowledgement of the inter-relationship between emotions, thought and behaviour has led to a cluster of behaviour intervention approaches which mainly address children's cognitive and emotional states to prevent and intervene with problem behaviours (Carpenter and Apter 1988). Nursery and primary school children, being at a developmental stage where their cognition is not highly developed, often do not know what is acceptable or what is expected from them. Sometimes they are not even aware that their behaviour is irritating and disturbing. Teachers then tend to adopt interventions which emphasise the important role of cognition and cognitive processes in the manifestation and change of overt behaviour (Kazdin 1990; Levis 1990; Kagan and Smith 1988; Fontana 1985). The cognitive approach actively employs cognitive processes for children's self-control of their own behaviour as opposed to the external control of behaviour, as happens with the conventional behavioural approaches (Bronson 2000; Carpenter and Apter 1988).

Social skills training

At the heart of the cognitive approach is the social skills training which enables children to (i) interpret social cues from others and the social context, (ii) develop social skills, (iii) be able to identify problems, predict solutions and generate alternatives and select and plan appropriate responses and (iv) use self-instruction and self-regulation (such as verbalising or speaking aloud what to do next) (Spence 2003). Instructions, guidance, rationales, modelling, and behaviour rehearsals are core elements in social skills training. Play offers an appropriate context in which all core elements of social training can be incorporated for children to practise identified social skills in an enjoyable manner rather than by using direct and didactic instruction (Spence 2003; Morgan and Jenson 1988; Fontana 1985).

Emotional literacy

An understanding of the link between an event, its interpretation and the emotions that follow is an important key to dealing with behaviour problems (Wilks 1998; Mayhew 1997; Goleman 1996). Therefore, affective variables such as feelings, emotions, thoughts and interpersonal relationships and the way they affect cognition started to be addressed in intervention programmes through 'emotional literacy' (Goleman 1997; Ingram and Scott 1990; Carpenter and Apter 1988). The notion of emotional literacy is not new. In the 1980s the idea of the affective education, which emphasized cognitive processes and emotions, had been introduced in the USA. However, at the time, affective education failed to make an impact in educational settings (Cooper-Epanchin and Monson 1982). The dominance of the behavioural approach which focused on observable and measurable behavioural outcomes together with the inherent difficulty of defining and measuring emotional states and affective variables became the main obstacles to the acceptance of affective education.

Since that time, more has become known about emotional literacy and the programmes developed have become more sophisticated in establishing the place of emotional literacy in educational settings (Goleman 1997). The aim is to help children to increase awareness and understanding of personal emotions and feelings and develop sensitivity to others through educational activities implemented in small developmental steps which provide positive feedback (Elliot and Place 1998; Carpenter and Apter 1988; Walker and Shea 1988). According to Weare and Gray (2003: 21–2), emotional literacy provides an 'organising framework for a range of work' which 'offers something positive for all children rather than specific action for those children demonstrating problems and difficulties.'

Circle time

Recently, circle time has been introduced into educational settings to help children to gain confidence and self-esteem. Circle time is the forum where children 'can have their say and be listened to' (Collins 2001: 7) and practise turn-taking, talking to the whole group, cooperating with children and adults, improving friend-making skills, identifying and expressing their needs and becoming aware of the needs of others. Topics such as knowing my strengths, my feelings, my senses, my body, my reactions, being with friends, quarrels and making up can be discussed with young children during circle time to address both feeling and emotions and social skills (Collins 2001; Sher 1998).

Although some techniques used in the cognitive approach seem to overlap with those used in the psychoeducational approach, still the cognitive approach is broader in the sense that it aims to deal with both the causes of a problem and the particular symptoms exhibited. Cognitive techniques seem also to be early years practitioners' and teachers' favourite techniques. Instructions and guidance, play and rehearsal as an essential part of any early years curriculum and settings, and meeting young children's developmental needs have been found to be the most frequently used techniques in nursery classes (Papatheodorou 1995). The main objection to the cognitive approach is that it is vague, imprecise and subjective, and individual teachers may give their own interpretations of children's problems, following an intervention plan that they think is the most appropriate (Fontana 1985).

The ecosystemic approach

The role of individuals' perceptions and interpretations of any given situation and behaviour are strongly emphasised in the ecosystemic approach. The assumption that individuals behave according to the way they interpret the situation becomes its basic principle. Often there is more than one valid interpretation for any particular situation. Therefore, changing the interpretation will lead to a change in behaviour. In turn, such changes in behaviour will influence others' perceptions and behaviour (Conoley and Carrington Rotto 1997; Cooper and Upton 1992; Molnar and Linquist 1989).

Reframing

Ecosystemic techniques are based on the principle of 'reframing' or 'divergent explanations' of problem behaviour (Molnar and Lindquist 1989). It is suggested that teachers and early years practitioners should re-examine specific problematic situations by re-defining behaviour problems, self-evaluate their own reactions to this behaviour and consider what purpose the behaviour serves for the pupil (Conoley and Carrington Rotto 1997).

Empathetic understanding

An empathetic understanding becomes the key feature in the ecosystemic approach. The use of empathy may help teachers to continually analyse the experience of schooling from the pupil's point of view. As Purkey and Novak (1984: 32) point out, 'What may be seen as illogical from an external point of view is only an inadequate understanding of what the world looks like from the internal viewpoint of the behaving person.' Importantly, Zabel (1988b) points out that approaching behaviour problems in this way requires teachers who themselves have achieved a high degree of maturity, who are well-adjusted, warm, objective and supportive.

Whole school/early years setting approaches

Ecosystemic techniques are addressed not only to individual children but to the whole system of the school/early years setting in which behaviour problems are exhibited. Educators' understanding of how contextual and situational events affect behaviour may provide important information on the basis of which intervention will then be planned, and provide important guidance for preventing or avoiding an unexpected crisis (Conoley and Carrington Rotto 1997; Cooper and Upton 1990, 1992). In the light of these assumptions, a whole-school/early years setting approach in dealing with children's problems is necessary. This approach focuses on the whole context of the school/early years setting and involves a radical examination of what it offers to all children and staff. It is responsive and supportive to the needs of both, and incorporates help from parents and the community (O'Brien 1998; Wilson 1998; Burden 1992).

At a theoretical level the ecosystemic approach seems to be more promising in dealing with behaviour problems, but there is little research support for its effectiveness. The conceptualisation of children's behaviour problems and relevant management approaches remains a proposed synthesis which needs to be further studied. However, the ecosystemic approach seems to provide a valuable addition to what has already been achieved by other behaviour management approaches (Cooper and Upton 1992).

An eclectic educational approach

In educational settings teachers seem not to be theory-oriented. Instead, they tend to employ and use whatever techniques have been proved to be effective and to work in their particular situation with their particular pupils. In general they use positive ways to deal with children's behaviour problems, but they do deliver punishment as well (Papatheodorou 2000). The ease with which management techniques can be applied in the classroom and the extent to which they meet children's developmental needs seem also to affect teachers' decisions about their usage (Papatheodorou 1995, 2000). Teachers also tend to avoid techniques that are complicated, time-consuming and require extra material for their application, as often happens with behavioural techniques (Schneider *et al.* 1992). In general, they tend to employ a variety of techniques of different theoretical orientation, indicating that their eclecticism is effect-based rather than theory-oriented (Papatheodorou 1995).

Teachers' and early years practitioners' eclecticism with regard to behaviour management techniques is likely to be an advantage as long as they do not allow one approach to confuse or contradict the other either in their own eyes or in those of their pupils (Fontana 1985). Indeed, such eclecticism seems to indicate that an integrated perspective which would consider both pupils' and teachers' experiences, and school pragmatics would be more promising than any approach discussed alone. The ecosystemic approach appears to present the framework where such eclecticism can have its place. Psychoeducational, behavioural and cognitive techniques can all be part of the ecosystemic approach which can ultimately provide a context for positive behaviour support.

Positive behaviour support

Positive behaviour support in educational settings aims to provide comprehensive interventions in naturalistic environments by reorganising a range of variables that have been identified as affecting behaviour, resulting in changes for both the individual child exhibiting problem behaviour and those persons who provide education and care to the child (Safran and Oswald 2003; Fox et al. 2002). Although positive behaviour support builds on the foundations of the behavioural approaches, it does adhere to a more positive, collaborative and holistic framework than behaviour change (Safran and Oswald 2003) to reflect the ethos and concepts underlying whole school/early years setting approaches (DfES 2002).

Positive behaviour support is based on the beliefs that (i) behind any difficult behaviour there is a reason, (ii) people should not control others, but should seek to support them by changing their own behaviour and (iii) neither coercion, nor interventions based on the aversive and punitive strategies once commonly incorporated in behaviour change and modification programmes, should be used to manage behaviour (Institute for Human Development Arizona 2004). Positive behaviour support applied within multiple environments and by multiple agents can result in powerful and durable behaviour change; based on 'open and respectful communication within the context of a support team [it] can provide the basis for understanding the familial and ecological features that are crucial to the origins and design of a comprehensive intervention' (Fox et al. 2002: 438).

In this context, early years practitioners and teachers should recognise that it is of particular importance to have a clear understanding of the techniques which they choose to address problem behaviours and such techniques should be consistent with and reflect the way they conceptualise and understand children's behaviour problems. In short, early years practitioners need to know and be clear why they choose the techniques they use. This point becomes particularly important for the early years professionals who are called on to play a vital role in the early identification and management of young children's behaviour problems (DfEE 1997, 1998).

Concluding remarks

For more than half a century there has been evidence of a shift from a purely psychoeducational approach that mainly addresses 'within-child' causes to a behavioural approach that addresses environmental factors that determine behaviour. As the behavioural approach tended to ignore children's cognition and feelings and did not take into account the multi-faceted nature of behaviour problems, both the cognitive and ecosystemic approaches came to make important contributions to these issues. In ecosystemic terms, although the child remains the focus of intervention strategies, these strategies move beyond the individual child to embrace environmental factors that promote and support positive behaviour.

Activity 7

- You may like to discuss with colleagues the approaches and techniques you use to deal with children's problem behaviours and examine their underlying principles.
- Consider whether there is a need for staff development activities and explain why.

Chapter 8

Screening and primary prevention

Early identification of potential behaviour problems

The case studies outlined in Chapter One show that potential problem behaviours may not be easily spotted and the factors associated with them are far from obvious. Young children's rapid and uneven changes make it difficult to form judgements about their behaviour and distinguish potentially persistent problems from transient ones. The overlapping nature of behaviour problems with other areas of development such as language and communication, motor skills and relationships and interactions with others further complicates the issue of early identification and assessment. The timing and the context in which such behaviours are exhibited reflect additional considerations for the early identification of young children's behavioural difficulties. In addition to these factors, the lack of consistent policies and practices across early childhood programmes and settings presents a barrier to early identification of behaviour problems. As a result, current systems for identifying, preventing and intervening with problem behaviours operate reactively, that is, after children have demonstrated significant and persistent behaviours lasting over a period of time (Conroy *et al.* 2001).

However, acknowledging these difficulties does not mean that the early identification of young children's potential behavioural difficulties is an impossible task. Early identification can be achieved by systematically applying informal and formal periodic screening and assessment procedures to examine children's well-being and holistic development in its immediate contexts (early years setting, home) by using a monitoring system that allows the recording and documentation of evidence. It must be noted here that screening and assessment are not interchangeable terms and carry out different functions in the process of early identification of behaviour problems.

Screening

Screening is a preliminary process applied to all children, to identify those who may be at risk of developing future behavioural difficulties in school and those who may already have such difficulties (Hills 1987), leading to actions which must be taken to either prevent or halt the progress of these difficulties before they become disturbing (Meisels and Atkins-Burnett 2000). Screening is based on the assumption that early identification and intervention are more effective, efficient and humane than letting problems escalate (Kauffman 1989). It typically provides a brief account of the child's present behaviour, described in terms of an observable event (Colmar 1988).

Screening usually, but not exclusively, includes checklists which have been devised as relatively quick and inexpensive tools that provide tentative indicators of children's development and behaviour and determine whether further assessment is required (Wilson 1998). Checklists do not intend 'to supply a prescription for "correct social behaviour", but rather to help teachers observe, understand and support all children as they grow in social skilfulness' (McClellan and Katz 1993: 2) and should not be used for grouping children for instructional purposes (Wilson 1998).

Checklists reflect maturational rather than transactional (interactive) models of development and often do not take into account contextual and cultural differences; their outcomes are also subject to how, when, and by and from whom information is obtained (Hills 1987). McClellan and Katz (1993) point out that individual children's distinct personalities and temperament, as well as family and cultural factors that may affect children's social behaviour, must be considered before arriving at any judgements about children's functioning and behaviour. However, Meisels and Atkins-Burnett (2000) argue that, for some time now, screening instruments have been available that demonstrate high sensitivity and specificity and there is growing evidence that screening can take place with substantial accuracy.

Issues in screening

If screening is adopted, early years practitioners need to establish good practice for screening procedures. Such practice requires that the children should be screened periodically over a period of time of approximately three to four weeks to make reasonably reliable judgements of the overall pattern of behaviour and functioning, and information should be collected from multiple sources and in situations and environments where children feel comfortable (e.g. playroom, classroom, home etc) (McClellan and Katz 1993; Hills 1987).

In addition, attention should be given to the facts that the purpose of screening should (i) be clear for early years practitioners and teachers, parents and all those involved in the process and (ii) be underpinned by sound ethical principles. Procedures adopted should also take into account developmental milestones associated with chronological age, life events and experiences, different environments and intervention strategies. The screening should be able to (i) eliminate common behaviour problems which do not carry serious consequences or are certain to resolve themselves without intervention, and (ii) identify children who are functioning at a developmental level inappropriate to their chronological age, and peers presenting additional challenges and for whom further support may be required. Finally, screening should be undertaken to identify children who need additional or different support, not to exclude them from existing programmes (Kauffman 1989; Hills 1987).

A blueprint for screening

Early years settings can establish systems of regular and systematic screening procedures that are developmentally appropriate to build up children's profiles and monitor their progress (Figure 8.1). It must be noted here that early years professionals should be kept informed about research that concerns screening tools, their adequacy and usefulness with particular groups of children (Hills 1987). Often, although checklists appear similar in content and purpose, they do not give comparable results (Ballard 1991). Thus, a sound checklist should be always accompanied by a rationale and user guide giving clear instructions for use and information on its limitations (Colmar 1988).

Screening for behaviour problems

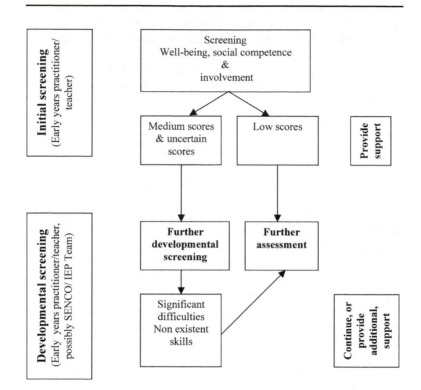

Figure 8.1 A blueprint for screening.

Class screening

Class screening should be undertaken regularly (preferably once during each term) to build up the profile of all children in the three dimensions of well-being, social competence and involvement (Form 8.1). Well-being, emotional competence and involvement are three dimensions which typify effective learners (Pascal 2003; Laevers *et al.* 1997, no date). Pascal (2003: 22) points out that these dimensions 'are not discrete but are intimately inter-related, each influencing and being influenced by, the others'.

Well-being refers to children's emotional development which 'enables the child to be assertive and to show and manage their emotions. They will also reflect peace, vitality and zeal for life and

Class screening

Class/EYs setting: *Date:*

Name	Emotional well-being	Social competence	Involvement
☐ Child 1	? L M H	? L M H	? L M H
☐ Child 2	? L M H	? L M H	? L M H
☐ Child 3	? L M H	? L M H	? L M H
☐ Child 4	? L M H	? L M H	? L M H
☐ Child 5	? L M H	? L M H	? L M H
☐ Child 6	? L M H	? L M H	? L M H
☐ Child 7	? L M H	? L M H	? L M H
☐ Child 8	? L M H	? L M H	? L M H
☐ Child 9	? L M H	? L M H	? L M H
☐ Child 10	? L M H	? L M H	? L M H
☐ Child 11	? L M H	? L M H	? L M H
☐ Child 12	? L M H	? L M H	? L M H
☐ Child 13	? L M H	? L M H	? L M H
☐ Child 14	? L M H	? L M H	? L M H
☐ Child 15	? L M H	? L M H	? L M H
☐ Child 16	? L M H	? L M H	? L M H

Form 8.1 Class screening (adapted from Laevers *et al.* no date).

will enjoy participating without too much anxiety' (Pascal 2003: 22). Signs of well-being include (Laevers *et al.* no date):

- children's adaptability and flexibility in their environment, situations and events;
- self-confidence and self-esteem reflected in the way the child faces new challenges, risking possible failure;
- assertiveness and ability to defend themselves, ask for help, support and comfort;
- vitality, level of energy expressed in their eyes, facial expression and posture;
- relaxation and inner peace reflected in flexible and smooth movements;
- enjoyment without restraints;
- ability to be in touch with own feelings, thoughts and needs and to express them.

Involvement, on the other hand, reflects the extent to which children are, or are not, involved in the activities undertaken in the classroom or any other setting (home, playgroup, playground etc). Involvement is not just about participation in activities, but rather 'intense engagement . . . intrinsically motivated' (Laevers *et al.* no date). Pascal (2003: 24) talks about attitudes and dispositions that are 'exhibited frequently in young children and in the absence of external coercion, threat or reward, which indicate internalised habits of mind under conscious and voluntary control'. Signs of involvement include (Laevers *et al.* no date):

- children's concentration reflected in a high level of absorption in an activity, absorption that can only be interrupted by intense external stimuli;
- energy, demonstrated in the effort and enthusiasm which they put into an activity or task;
- creative and complex involvement in new and challenging situations, apart from routine activities;
- body-language, facial expression and composure which show deep involvement;
- persistence, whereby they neither give up easily, nor are tempted by easier tasks or activities;
- precision, reflected in the children's care over the work;

- time taken for children to react to new stimuli, showing motivation;
- verbal expression that shows their involvement and satisfaction and pleasure.

Social competence is defined as 'the ability of the child to reach out to others and to make connections and relationships that help them to survive and thrive' (Pascal 2003: 23). Signs of social competence include (Pascal 2003: 23) the ability:

- to initiate interaction, to cooperate with others, accept others' ideas and suggestions and share experiences;
- to show empathy, consideration and respect towards the feelings and intentions of others;
- to take responsibility for one's own actions, which shows a developing sense of right and wrong;
- to show assertiveness by communicating and negotiating their opinions and ideas and offering suggestions;
- to have a sense of belonging and personal identity.

Record keeping

A colour-coded representation of the screening findings can give a quick overview of the profile of all children. Green, orange and red colours (or any other preferred colours) may be used next to each child's name (Form 8.1) to represent high, medium and uncertain scores, and low scores, respectively. Uncertain scores are indicated by a question mark (Laevers *et al.* no date). Children who receive low and/or medium scores or uncertain judgements should undergo further developmental screening, while children who have low scores should be immediately referred for a more systematic and in-depth assessment (to be discussed in Chapter Nine). In both cases, immediate action is required through the early years programme by either differentiating the learning outcomes for individual children needing support and/or by differentiating the play and learning activities to achieve expected outcomes.

   The results of successive class screening can be summarised to obtain an overview of the profile of the class/early years setting in each term and the progress made over time. Considering screening to have taken place in October, February and May in a class of sixteen children, successive screening results may show a pattern

Screening date	Class profile and progress (no. of children)		
	☐ (red)	☐ (orange)	☐ (green)
October	3	5	8
February	1	4	11
May	1	3	12

Form 8.2 Successive class screening results (adapted from Laevers *et al.* no date).

such as that in Form 8.2. Class screening is a useful tool (i) to identify any common patterns in the three dimensions of well-being, social competence and involvement across all children and (ii) to obtain an initial profile of individual children who may need either further development screening and/or assessment. Screening information should be used to plan an appropriate curriculum for all children and not to place individual children on any intervention programmes.

Further developmental screening

Considering that in young children behaviour problems are often developmentally related (Papatheodorou 1995) and the result of not yet fully developed cognitive, language, communication and motor skills, for children whose scores are low or medium or judgements are uncertain, it is important to establish their performance and outcomes in these areas. Information from developmental screening may provide specific 'cues' for the potential factors that may contribute to children's problem behaviours (Watson and Steege 2003; McComas *et al.* 2000).

The assessment scales, and especially those referring to personal, social and emotional development, communication and language, and physical development, provided by the Foundation Stage Profile (DfES and QCA 2003), may be used to build up the profile of children who received medium scores or for whom it was difficult to make definite judgements about their performance in the class screening. The assessment scales have not been developed to identify children's problem behaviours, nor to make judgements about children's level of development; however, their regular use allows for the identification of children's strengths and difficulties, as they are witnessed in a naturalistic environment where children are engaged in play and learning activities, and provides cues for potential problem behaviours.

Wilson's (1998) checklist for 'pragmatic skills' is another tool that can be used for 'fine grained' screening of children's cognitive, speech and communication skills (Form 8.3). The checklist allows the assessment of different aspects of the receptive and expressive areas of language, that is, attending to language, listening and comprehension (receptive area) and communicative functions, conversational competence and social skills (expressive area). Behaviours are rated on a scale 1 to 5, with 1 showing no need for improvement and 5 indicating non-existent behaviours. Scores which show non-existent skills or skills needing critical improvement require further assessment of children.

Interpretation and use of screening information

By its nature, screening information is limited and does not provide the 'whole picture' (Wilson 1998) of the child as might have emerged through systematic assessment which also considers situational and contextual factors. Screening information should be only seen as an indication of potential difficulties which may place children at risk of developing behaviour problems and threaten their well-being, and should be used to plan activities which, implemented systematically and consistently, may counteract such difficulties.

Emotional literacy for primary prevention

Emotional literacy has been a key goal in providing 'primary prevention' (Goleman 1997: xiii), addressing children's needs which are not of immediate consideration (Bryer 1988). It offers a framework for integrating emotional and social competencies into the culture and curricula of educational settings by teaching children in a developmentally appropriate way over a sustained period of time (Goleman 1997). In the early years where 'services should be

Child .... Birthday.........................

Person completing form .... Relationship to the child.........................

Date.........................

Key: 1 *Needs no improvement* 2 *Acceptable* 3 *Needs improvement* 4 *Critical need for improvement* 5 *Non-existent*

RECEPTIVE AREA

1. Attending behavior

Makes eye contact	1	2	3	4	5
Maintains attention to speaker	1	2	3	4	5

2. Auditory listening skills

Attends to sounds	1	2	3	4	5
Responds to sounds	1	2	3	4	5
Localizes source of sounds	1	2	3	4	5
Listens actively to sounds	1	2	3	4	5
Attends to significant auditory information in presence of background noises (*selective attention*)	1	2	3	4	5
Maintains attention over a period of time (*sustained attention*)	1	2	3	4	5

3. Comprehension of meaning

'Reads' typical nonverbal cues (*e.g., frowns, gestures*)	1	2	3	4	5
Carries out requests or commands	1	2	3	4	5

Understands much of what is said to him or her (i.e., relates spoken language to what it represents) | 1 | 2 | 3 | 4 | 5

Understands much of what is said to him or her (i.e., relates spoken language to what it represents)	1	2	3	4	5
Understands verbal hints (implied messages)	1	2	3	4	5
Understands questions	1	2	3	4	5
Interprets environmental sounds	1	2	3	4	5

EXPRESSIVE AREA

1. Communicative functions

Imitates sounds	1	2	3	4	5
Requests assistance	1	2	3	4	5
Requests information (i.e., asks appropriate questions)	1	2	3	4	5
Uses directive speech (e.g., commands, threats)	1	2	3	4	5
Expresses desires	1	2	3	4	5
Uses the names of objects, events, etc.	1	2	3	4	5
Formulates questions	1	2	3	4	5
Offers assistance	1	2	3	4	5
Disagrees verbally or argues	1	2	3	4	5
Justifies own actions (i.e., gives reasons)	1	2	3	4	5
Recognizes problems and offers solutions	1	2	3	4	5
Makes self understood (i.e., is able to get a point across)	1	2	3	4	5

2. Conversational competence

Uses good voice habits (i.e., neither loud nor too soft)	1	2	3	4	5

continued on next page

Answers questions	1	2	3	4	5
Talks about experiences	1	2	3	4	5
Varies speech according to setting and other speakers	1	2	3	4	5
Acknowledges what another speaker has said	1	2	3	4	5
Demonstrates appropriate turn-taking behaviour	1	2	3	4	5
Initiates conversational topics	1	2	3	4	5
Makes conversational transitions in an appropriate manner	1	2	3	4	5
Participates willingly in social conversations	1	2	3	4	5
Makes suggestions and shares ideas	1	2	3	4	5
Provides sufficient (but not too much) information when answering questions	1	2	3	4	5
Communicates about self	1	2	3	4	5
Communicates about things outside self (i.e., describes objects)	1	2	3	4	5
Communicates about concrete experiences	1	2	3	4	5
Communicates abstract ideas	1	2	3	4	5
Describes an object or explains how something works	1	2	3	4	5
Tells a simple story in proper sequence	1	2	3	4	5

3. Social interactive skills

Expresses feelings in socially acceptable ways	1	2	3	4	5
Honors established social conventions	1	2	3	4	5
Adapts a message to the social context	1	2	3	4	5
Initiates contact	1	2	3	4	5
Responds to contact	1	2	3	4	5
Engages in interactive play	1	2	3	4	5

Form 8.3 Checklist of pragmatic skills (reprinted from Wilson 1998 with kind permission).

promoted as a positive resource . . . and a mechanism for promoting the well-being of children' (Mental Health Foundation no date: 13), emotional literacy becomes of particular importance especially in the way the curriculum is implemented. In addition, considering that often curricular demands may be the source of at least some of children's problem behaviours, it is of importance to counteract such problems by embracing emotional literacy.

Emotional literacy for emotional and social competencies and self-regulation

The interplay between emotions, cognition and behaviour has been an important factor in supporting the development of emotional and social competencies (Goleman 1997) which are considered fundamental for self-regulation (Bronson 2000) (Figure 8.2). Self-regulation is understood as the child's ability to manage his/her own feelings, thoughts and actions in adaptive and flexible ways across a variety of social or physical contexts (Saarni 1997: 39) and reflects the belief that children should develop inner rather than externally imposed discipline (Porter 2003; Konopka 2002). Self-regulation, however, is also determined by other areas of development such as physical maturation, sensori-motor development and cognitive development (Bronson 2000) (Figure 8.2). This, to some extent, may explain the observed overlap between young children's problem behaviours and developmentally related problems (Papatheodorou 1995).

In young children, the interrelationship between social and emotional competencies and the underdeveloped or developing physical, motor and cognitive development necessitates 'an integrated approach that considers the "Whole Child" to achieve self-regulation' (Bronson 2000: 6). Emotional literacy can become the home of a range of behaviour management strategies which, being organised in a comprehensive and sequential manner, offer young children the opportunity to develop emotional and social competencies (Defalco 1997).

Exploring feelings

Literature plays an important role in personal development, and storytelling, in particular, is crucial in young children's development and understanding of self and others through the powers of

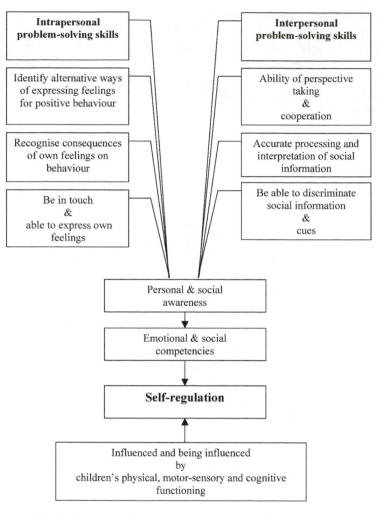

Figure 8.2 Social and emotional competencies and self-regulation.

imagination and mythic thinking and a sense of magic and awe (Papatheodorou and Gill 2002). Stories depict experiences of life in a structured and organised way, perpetuate knowledge, and offer instructions and guidance, shelter and healing (Harper and Gray 1997).

Literature is also part of all curricula in educational settings and as such forms the basis for emotional literacy. Stories from books, personal stories or pictures, illustrations, posters and filmstrips can be used to offer children the opportunity to be introduced to a number of situations and social events to evoke a range of feelings and emotions. Children, through careful discussions, can explore and name the feelings of the characters, developing, at the same time, an appropriate vocabulary. Further discussion may help children to understand what made the characters of the story feel the way they did (explore antecedents), how they reacted or coped in response to their feelings, and to recognise the physical signs of feelings (facial expressions and body language), what the results of their behaviour were (explore consequences), and how the characters could better have dealt with their feelings (problem solving/providing alternatives) (Papatheodorou and Gill 2001). In this way, instructions, guidance and rationales become an integral part of the storytelling process that helps children in personal and social awareness in a non-personalised way. Circle time may be used to discuss in a structured manner and in a safe environment a number of problem-solving situations that come out of the stories and are confronted by most young children (Collins 2001; Sher 1998). Early years practitioners and teachers may like to go a step further and allow children to relate the story to their own experiences and discuss relevant issues (Dowling 2000). However, attention must be drawn to the fact that this is not an easy task. Early years practitioners and teachers must be feeling confident that they have already established an emotionally safe environment in their settings and are confident in their skills at handling the unexpected and unsettling situations which may arise from such activities.

Limitations imposed by language

Considering the level of young children's language and communication skills, discussions may limit the experiences of children. Even fully developed language and communication skills may not be adequate to illustrate many of the feelings experienced by children. Jacoby (1999: 53) argues that 'language is a double-edged sword. On the one hand, it enriches the field of common experience; on the other hand, it limits it. Only part of the original, global experience can be expressed in words. The rest remains inaccurately named and poorly understood.' Here is where stories can be brought to life and relived by the children through role play, rehearsals and modelling and by incorporating expressive arts (e.g. music, movement and dance) to give children the opportunity to imitate the characters of the story, model their feelings and actions and sometimes 'rewrite' the story to explore alternative feelings, behaviours and actions.

Story playing

Through carefully planned and implemented programmes of emotional literacy children become personally and socially aware and develop emotional and social competencies. At the same time, by incorporating role play, rehearsals and modelling, stories become the forum for social skills training, language and communication support and physical and motor development (Figure 8.3). In this way, storytelling and story playing offer first-hand experience for children to access their own and others' feelings and thoughts, exercise rationality by exploring the emotional antecedents and consequences of behaviour, acquire social and coping skills through rehearsals, modelling and role play, and problem-solving skills by providing alternative solutions (Papatheodorou 2004; Ingram and Scott 1990).

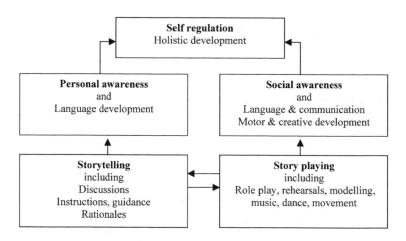

Figure 8.3 Storytelling and story playing for emotional and social competencies.

Issues in emotional literacy

When emotional literacy is employed to address certain difficulties experienced by individual children, it is of importance that early years practitioners and teachers get to know the individual children, show empathy for their needs and develop positive relationships. In devising emotional literacy programmes, early years practitioners should remember that feelings and emotions exist in the context of other personal characteristics and interpersonal relationships which are subject to cultural differences, and sometimes sharing experiences in a group situation may not be suitable for all children (Cooper-Epanchin and Monson 1982). Early years practitioners and teachers need to know when and how to intervene, as well as to be aware of their own limitations and to ask for support from colleagues and other professionals, if necessary.

Therefore, it is important that emotional literacy is fitted into existing structures of the early years settings and integrated within the regular play and curriculum activities. Emotional literacy activities should start with impersonal, neutral and group-oriented activities, evaluated for their appropriateness for all children and individually respecting their right to privacy. Through emotional literacy children should be taught what they can and should do, rather than being criticised (Cooper-Epanchin and Monson 1982). A clear definition and understanding of the conceptual framework of emotional literacy and its integration into current theory and research of child development are two factors that ultimately affect the successful implementation of emotional literacy. The early years practitioners' and teachers' personality and behaviour are also equally important factors (Carpenter and Apter 1988).

Concluding remarks

Screening is a preliminary process undertaken periodically over a period of time to identify children at risk of developing behaviour problems. Children whose behaviour has been identified as being of concern should undergo further developmental screening and, if necessary, further assessment to consider contextual factors. Screening should inform the development and implementation of curricular activities that address the particular needs of the children attending the early years setting. Emotional literacy is a medium of addressing young children's developing emotional and social competencies to achieve self-regulation.

 Activity 8

- Examine the existing screening system in your setting, if you have one, and state how you use it, how often and for what purpose.
- If you do not have one, discuss with colleagues the possibility of introducing one, considering the implications for staff and other resources.

Chapter 9

Assessment of behaviour problems

Issues in assessment

Severe problem behaviours and problem behaviours which are frequent, last for some time and do not improve with the support provided require further detailed and systematic assessment (Campell 2002; Ballard 1991; Hills 1987). Assessment is usually undertaken by professionals with particular knowledge, skills, competencies and expertise such as Special Educational Needs Coordinators (SENCOs) or Individual Educational Plan (IEP) teams. In cases where the child's behaviour is severe enough and/or situational and contextual factors are too complex to be dealt with through the resources available to the early years setting, professionals with specialist knowledge and psychological services may be involved. A few cases may be referred for statutory assessment. However, in all cases the early years practitioner/teacher should remain an active participant in the process (DfES 2001a; Watson and Steege 2003; Quinn et al. 1998).

Assessment is defined as 'a process in which various strategies are used to evaluate child learning and development, including evaluation of cultural, social and physical contexts within which learning and development occurs' (Ballard 1991: 127). Assessment aims to help professionals and early years practitioners to 'know' the child through a process of systematically gathering data (Wilson 1998: 159). Until recently, assessment involved predominantly psychometric, normative standardised tests which focused exclusively on the characteristics of the child (Shapiro and Kratochwill 2000). Considering that behaviour is interactive and subject to dynamic social interrelationships and processes, a single normative test is of little value as (i) it does not offer the contextual information required and (ii) the labelling that usually emerges from such testing, apart from its stigmatising effects, has little to offer in designing intervention strategies and programmes (Ballard 1991).

Current thinking about assessment has moved beyond the individual child to include assessment of contextual factors, their interrelationships and the way in which they influence the child's behaviour (Ballard 1991). Assessment does not only aim to describe symptomatic behaviour, but also attempts 'to unravel the various factors that have played a part in the causation of any particular problem or difficulty' (DoH, DfEE and HO 2000: 69). Such factors include any immediate and distant events that preceded (antecedents) and follow (consequences) a child's behaviour and the relationships and interactions developed in any of the contexts such as early years setting/school, family and community. An appreciation of the interrelatedness of these variables also contributes to a better understanding of the behaviour exhibited (Shapiro and Kratochwill 2000; Neisworth and Bagnato 1988).

Ballard (1991: 130) points out that those who are involved in the assessment process need to be aware of any 'collateral outcomes' which are defined as 'the effects which were not intended as part of an action, but that may be more significant than the intended outcomes themselves'. Collateral outcomes may be either positive or negative. For instance, understanding and acceptance of cultural differences may have a positive effect on the assessment process and its outcomes, whereas low expectations due to preconceived ideas about children's emotional state and social skills may lead to negative outcomes.

Different types of assessment

Functional assessment

In the 1980s the growing dissatisfaction which emerged from the use of psychometric normative tests led to functional assessment, which focuses on the functions and purpose which behaviour serves and the factors that trigger or sustain such behaviour (Watson and Steege 2003; Gimpel and Holland 2003). Functional behavioural assessment is based on the belief that all behaviour serves a purpose and whereas behaviour may be judged as inappropriate, its function may not be so. Therefore, the best way to change behaviour is to understand its functions and the reasons behind it.

Functional behavioural assessment is defined as a systematic process which aims (i) to describe difficult behaviour, (ii) identify its functions and purpose, (iii) investigate environmental factors and setting events that predict such behaviour and (iv) guide the development of effective intervention programmes (Institute for Human Development Arizona 2004; Watson and Steege 2003; Quinn *et al.* 1998). Functional assessment is conceptualised as a problem-solving process that looks beyond the behaviour itself to understand *why* a child is misbehaving, and what the *functions, purpose* and *causes* of the behaviour exhibited are (Gimpel and Holland 2003; Watson and Steege 2003; Quinn *et al.* 1998).

Functional assessment reflects an important shift in the focus of assessment, to highlight that, for instance, two children who exhibit similar behaviour may do so for completely different reasons. A child may constantly fail to undertake or complete certain activities and tasks and become distractive, or run away to avoid the task, because s/he has not acquired the skills required. Another child, however, may display the same behaviour because s/he has learned to get individual attention and support from the early years practitioner or teacher. Direct observation may be the appropriate way to identify the trigger of the observed behaviour in the former instance but not in the latter, which may require different methods such as discussion with the child and/or his/her parents. However, Quinn *et al.* (1998) point out that 'a single source of information . . . does not produce sufficiently accurate information, especially if the problem behaviour serves several functions that vary according to circumstances'. For example, the child may refuse to participate in certain activities either because s/he has not acquired the skills or because of low self-esteem and fear that s/he will fail the task. Therefore, it is important to bear in mind that 'contextual factors are more than the sum of observable behaviours' as they may include less obvious parameters such as the affective and cognitive elements which affect explicit behaviour (Rolls 1999; Quinn *et al.* 1998; Carpenter and Apter 1988).

Ecological assessment

The existing understanding of behaviour as being a function of the dynamic interrelationships of the individual and contextual variables has led to the notion of ecological assessment which refers to 'the examination and recording of the physical, social, and psychological features of a child's developmental context' (Neisworth and Bagnato 1988: 39). Physical elements include room and classroom layout, quantity and quality of resources and play materials available, lighting and temperature. Social and psychological factors include peer interaction, friendships and relationships established with other children and adults. In addition, sensitivity, responsiveness and respect for family structures and child-rearing practices due to culture, religion and ethnic origin should ensure equal opportunities. Similarly, socio-economic influences on children's well-being and behaviour should be examined and any conclusions should be interrogated to avoid the biases of individuals' preconceived and, sometimes, judgemental and stereotypical views (DoH, DfEE and HO 2000).

Multidimensional assessment

The acknowledgement of the complexities of human development and behaviour requires assessment methodologies and information collection to reflect such complexities. Information collected with one method, from one particular source over specific behaviours is neither better nor more accurate than data collected with different methods, from different sources (Shapiro and Kratochwill 2000). Instead assessment should be based on a multidimensional model which, according to Neisworth and Bagnato (1988), refers to 'a comprehensive and integrated evaluation approach that employs *multiple measures*, derives data from *multiple sources*, surveys *multiple domains* and fulfils *multiple purposes*' (p. 24).

Multiple measures may combine direct (observations) and indirect (interviews, documents) methods of collecting information. The multi-source aspect of assessment requires that information is gathered from several contexts such as early years setting/school, home and from different and multiple sources (early years practitioners/teachers, parents and other professionals, if and when required) (Meisels and Atkins-Burnett 2000). Multi-domain assessment requires that information is gathered not only about the child's difficulties, but about his/her strengths and capabilities as well (DfES 2001a; DoH, DfEE and HO 2000). Multi-purpose assessment refers to the several functions which assessment should fulfil, that is, (i) describing problem behaviour, (ii) determining the functions of the behaviour, (iii) informing the planning of intervention and (iv) monitoring and evaluating intervention (Neisworth and Bagnato 1988).

Play-based assessment

The importance of collecting situational and contextual information to determine the functions and possible causes of behaviour has led to the requirement for assessment to take place in naturalistic, non-threatening environments where children are involved in naturally evolving play and learning activities (Meisels and Atkins-Burnett 2000). For young children, assessment became 'play-based' (Sayeed and Guerin 2000; Sheridan et al. 1995) and children's behaviour started to be observed and systematically recorded in all forms of play such as role play, pretend play, rehearsals, group play and solitary play (Sayeed and Guerin 2000; Neisworth and Bagnato 1988). According to Sheridan et al. (1995), play offers clues which reveal children's skills and abilities as they attempt to make sense of, and negotiate, the world around them. Play-based assessment does not only provide information about children's current functioning, but also about their emerging competencies and skills. It offers information about how children are doing things and in this way enables better use of resources to support children's potential for future development (Meisels and Atkins-Burnett 2000).

Play-based assessment has moved away from normative assessment to embrace criterion-referenced assessment. Whereas normative assessment compares an individual child's behaviour against the norms expected for children of the same age, criterion-referenced assessment examines the child's current behaviour and, at the same time, identifies the skills and strategies which the child needs in order to achieve expected behaviours (Pretti-Frontczak et al. 2002; Sayeed and Guerin 2000). Although the child is at the centre of the process, play-based and criterion-referenced assessment move beyond the child to examine the way situational and contextual factors may need to be manipulated for the child to achieve expected behaviours.

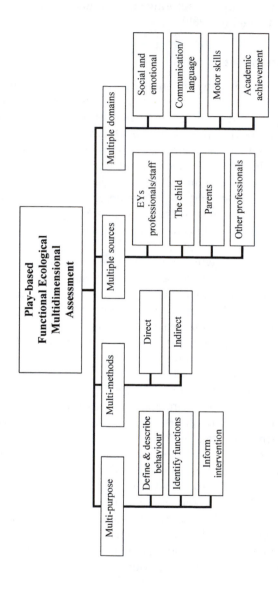

Figure 9.1 An integrated model of play-based, functional, ecological and multidimensional assessment.

Towards an integrated model of assessment

Existing understanding of behaviour and developments regarding conceptual frameworks about assessment highlight the importance of adopting and using an integrated model of assessment to identify problems behaviours in young children (Figure 9.1). This model of assessment allows behaviour to be defined and described in operational terms making its purpose and functions explicit (functional assessment), requires interrelationships and contextual factors to be investigated (ecological assessment), serves multiple purposes by using multiple methods, uses multiple sources for information to be collected from multiple domains (multi-dimensional assessment) and it is play-based as it is carried out in naturalistic environments.

A blueprint for assessment

Assessment requires a sequence of structured procedures that allow the collection, recording and systematic monitoring of objective and quantifiable data in order to measure behaviour and make informed decisions about intervention (Figure 9.2). Information can be obtained from a variety of contexts to represent multiple perspectives about the child's difficulties as well as to access the strengths and capacities of such different perspectives (Meisels and Atkins-Burnett 2000).

Collecting information

According to Meisels and Atkins-Burnett (2000: 233), assessment begins with 'the establishment of reliable, working alliances with significant individuals in the child's life', as these individuals hold important information about the child's behaviour in different contexts. Interviews with parents and family members may provide useful information about the type and frequency of problem behaviour, contextual factors and how these may influence behaviour and the strengths and capabilities of the child (Institute for Human Development Arizona 2004; Quinn et al. 1998). However, before the collection of any information, it is important to establish mutual trust and respect, to have an understanding of the family's own circumstances, strengths and challenges, and to clarify any

Assessment of Behaviour Problems

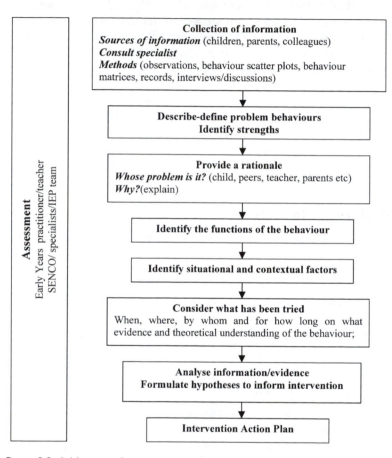

Figure 9.2 A blueprint for an integrated model of assessment for behaviour problems.

cultural assumptions underpinning assessment (Meisels and Atkins-Burnett 2000).

To make sense of 'everyday life events' (Garfat 2002), discussions with the child are useful in examining the child's own perception of the situation or events: that is, what s/he thought happened before and after the particular incidents, how s/he felt before and after the incident, and what else could have been done (Quinn *et al.* 1998).

Information can also be gathered indirectly by reviewing records which may provide general facts about the child (e.g. health problems, allergies, hearing, vision etc), additional information about his/her behaviour across different settings, background information about his/her family (family composition, circumstances, exceptional events etc) and wider community and neighbourhood (socio-economic conditions, disadvantage, services, facilities etc).

Methods of collecting information

Observations and systematic recording of the incidence of children's behaviour within naturalistic environments (e.g. home, classroom, playground) are useful tools to identify situational factors that affect or determine behaviour (McComas et al. 2000; Quinn et al. 1998). Observations can be continuous and uninterrupted over a specified period of time in a particular context to produce a descriptive narrative account (Neisworth and Bagnato 1988). Observations should focus purely on the description of overt behaviour and situational events, and any interpretations of, and/or judgements on, the child's behaviour must be separately recorded to be used in the analysis (making sense) of the information gathered (Watson and Steege 2003; Quinn et al. 1998) (see Form 9.1).

Once the presence of certain behaviours has been established and described in concrete terms, the frequency, continuity, severity and the patterns of such behaviours should be determined. For instance, specific behaviours may occur during particular days of the week and in specific activities, but not in others. Sampling is a useful method of recording observations to establish these conditions. Sampling involves systematic observations and recording of information regarding specific behaviours (e.g. social engagement, communication, collaboration, fights, arguments) and within pre-specified intervals (moments in time) to record behaviour across different times of the day over a period of time (Form 9.2) and during a range of activities (lunchtime, playtime, group activities, story time etc) (Form 9.3).

Systematic multiple methods of observation allow early years practitioners/teachers to (i) describe the child's behaviour, measure its frequency and identify any patterns occurring, (ii) document whether a concern about the child's behaviour is based on actual facts rather than initial perceptions and judgements, (iii) determine

Observation Form

Continuous descriptive record

Child's name:

Activity:

Date:

Any additional information:

Observer's name:

Behaviour to be observed (if applicable):

Time:

Description of behaviour (What has been heard and seen)	Potential initial judgements and interpretations (Feelings at the time of observing and recording data)	Analysis of observational data (Identify Antecedents Behaviour – Consequences)
This column contains a description of the events and behaviour exhibited in concrete terms (e.g. Child A pushed child B. Child B pushed child A with force. Child A smacked child B. Child B cries. Teacher told child A off and moved him/her on to another activity. Child B is comforted).	This column may include comments about the observer's feeling and judgements made during the observation (such as early years professional is unfair; child A is naughty; child B is frustrated etc).	This column must be used to state the antecedents and consequences of the behaviour and whether further information is required.

Form 9.1 Continuous descriptive observations.

Observation Form
Assessment Scatter Plot

Child's name: *Date: 1/03 to 19/03 2005*

Observer's name: *Time: 9.00–12.35*

Activity:

Behaviour to be observed: (e.g. arguments, fights, tantrums, oppositional behaviour, non-compliance, other)

☐ No behaviour   ▨ Low rates of behaviour   ■ High rates of behaviour

Time	Dates									
	1/03	2/03	3/03	4/03	5/03	15/03	16/03	17/03	18/03	19/03
9.00-9.05										
9.30-9.35										
10.00-10.05										
10.30-10.35										
11.00-11.05										
12.00-12.05										
12.30-12.35										

Form 9.2 Assessment scatter plot form (adapted from Quinn *et al.* 1998).

Note
The scatter plot can be modified:
i. to include the behaviours that are of concern for individual children;
ii. to define the period of time that is required to establish whether there are any patterns of problem behaviour.

situational or location factors that affect behaviour and (iv) inform the planning of intervention programmes and resources and materials required (Neisworth and Bagnato 1988).

Describing and defining problem behaviour – identifying strengths

Assessment requires that behaviour is described in concrete terms that are understood by, and easily communicated with, all those involved in the assessment process (Quinn *et al.* 1998). Generic terms such as child A is withdrawn, child B is aggressive and child C has poor social skills shed little light on the child's observed

Observation Form
Assessment Matrix

Child's name: *Date: 1/03/2005*

Observer's name: *Time: 9.00–12.35*

Behaviour to be observed: (e.g. arguments, fights, tantrums, oppositional behaviour, non-compliance, other)

☐ No behaviour   ▦ Low rates of behaviour   ■ Persistent behaviour

Behaviours	Free play	Structured play/activities	Instructional play/games	Outdoor play	Lunchtime	Small group	Large group	Story time	Reading	Writing activities
Arguments										
Fights										
Tantrums										
Oppositional behaviour										
Non-compliance										
Other (specify)										
Other (specify)										

Form 9.3 Assessment matrix (adapted from Quinn *et al.* 1998).

Note
The matrix form can be modified to include:
i. the behaviours that are of concern for individual children;
ii. the range and nature of activities undertaken in particular early years
    settings.

behaviour. Instead it is important that behaviour is described by identifying specific behaviours and acts, that is, child A avoids other children, starts crying when s/he is asked to join group activities, child B pulls other children's hair, bites and kicks them etc, child C cannot share toys, negotiate play, follow rules etc.

Description of behaviour in concrete and operational terms allows (i) measuring of its frequency (how often the behaviour is exhibited), duration (how long it lasts) and severity (how serious it is and for whom), (ii) identification of any occurring patterns, that is, whether the behaviour is happening in isolation or in conjunction with other behaviours, (iii) identification of the timing (what time and during what part of the day it is happening) and location (where it is happening) of the behaviour as well as others involved in the incident. The use of assessment scatter plots (Form 9.2) and behaviour matrices (Form 9.3) to record observations are useful tools for determining such factors.

Assessment should also consider the child's strengths (e.g. personal characteristics, predispositions and skills), emerging competencies and the positive features existing within the natural environment where behaviour occurs (Watson and Steege 2003; DoH, DfEE and HO 2000; Quinn et al. 1998). Identifying the child's strengths and positive characteristics of the child and the environment are important personal and ecological resources which intervention programmes can call upon or utilise to support the child (Meisels and Atkins-Burnett 2000).

Providing a rationale

The definition and description of a child's behaviour is followed by a rationale as to why such behaviour is judged to be difficult and/or problematic. Often behaviours that are significant for one member of staff are insignificant for others. Some issues which the assessment team should consider include the extent to which the behaviour interferes with and affects the child's own and other children's well-being, learning and development and whether all members of staff have equal concerns. It is important to remember that individual expectations about behaviour may differ considerably among people depending on their implicit and explicit personal and professional values and beliefs (Institute for Human Development Arizona 2004; Campbell 2002).

Identifying the functions of the behaviour

The next step of the assessment process involves the identification of the purpose and functions of the behaviour. The same behaviour may serve completely different functions for the child, for example (i) gaining social attention, (ii) having access to activities, resources, tangible rewards etc, (iii) avoiding something such as activities that may be uninteresting, tiring or do not match the child's skills and competencies) and (iv) receiving automatic visual, auditory and haptic stimulation (McComas *et al.* 2000; Quinn *et al.* 1998). Some behaviour may not be clearly explained in terms of the functions it serves and as such may require that its causes be established. Behaviour often appears not to be mediated by its social and sensory consequences, which can be observed directly, but to be related to 'private events' such as thoughts and feelings that are not directly observable (Watson and Steege 2003: 38).

A detailed, fine-grained analysis of the information collected from multiple sources often reveals that, although some behaviours are the consequences of multiple and complex factors, environmental factors and setting arrangements tend to reinforce them further (Watson and Steege 2003; Neisworth and Bagnato 1988). For example, a child who is not involved in activities because of fear of failing may start to engage if curricular and setting arrangements provide opportunities for successful outcomes. Having gained confidence with his/her engagement in simple tasks, the child may gradually move towards more complex and demanding tasks.

Identifying situational and contextual factors

As the behaviour is not happening in isolation, it is important to identify those contextual variables and events that contribute to such behaviour. Questions to be asked include: where and when is the behaviour more likely to occur? Does the behaviour raise concerns across different contexts and situations? What has preceded (antecedents) and followed (consequences) the behaviour? Who else has been involved? How is the daily programme organised and structured? Is the daily programme too unpredictable? What are the activities and expectations? How is the physical environment organised? What is the level of noise, temperature and light? Is it more likely that 'bad' behaviour is noticed rather than 'good' behaviour?

Establishing what has been tried

It has already been stated that when initial concerns are raised about a child's well-being and behaviour, early years practitioners/teachers should take immediate action and provide support on the basis of existing knowledge. A good assessment also seeks to learn from the past by recording what has been done so far, when, where, by whom and for how long and whether it has worked or not (Institute for Human Development Arizona 2004; Bryer 1988).

Analysing information and formulating hypotheses

Information collected needs to be analysed, interpreted and used to formulate hypotheses about the behaviours exhibited. The information should neither be used to label the child or place him/her in an 'identified category' of behaviour problems (e.g. ADHD, bullying, depression) and then identify intervention programmes that are deemed appropriate for such behaviours, nor to predict future performance (Wilson 1998). Instead analysis requires an interrogation of information in the light of existing knowledge (theories) to tentatively formulate hypotheses (that is, probable explanations) about the functions of problem behaviour and possible factors associated with them, and the way they can be controlled to eliminate their effect on the behaviour (McComas *et al.* 2000; Quinn *et al.* 1998).

It is important to note here that the personal and professional philosophy and the attitudes and values of all those involved in the process of assessment are influential factors which contribute to the way the information collected is interpreted. Therefore, the analysis and interpretation of the information should not be undertaken as only one person's task but rather collectively, to examine multiple perspectives and interpretations. In addition, as Wilson (1998: 172) points out, consideration must be given to the fact that information collected does not represent a 'total picture' of the child's behaviour but rather 'a picture in time', a snapshot. Therefore, such 'pictures' should not be used to make predictions about the child's future behaviour.

Devising an intervention action plan

According to Meisels and Atkins-Burnett (2000), assessment is the beginning of intervention. The information collected during assessment is summarised to devise an intervention action plan (Laevers *et al.* no date) which, regardless of its format, states (i) the problem behaviour and the child's strengths, (ii) the situational and contextual factors that may contribute to problem behaviour, (iii) hypotheses regarding the functions of the behaviour and (iv) the goals and objectives expected to be achieved through planned intervention (Form 9.4). Consequently, the intervention action plan informs the planning for an 'individually tailored' behaviour intervention plan (to be discussed in the next chapter) which meets and caters for the particular needs of the child (Watson and Steege 2003: 143).

Principles underpinning assessment

The model of assessment outlined above does not aim to tell practitioners which particular methods to use in given situations or to set out a formula that can be applied in all circumstances. Instead it aims to provide a framework for a systematic way of collecting, recording, analysing and understanding children's behaviour within and between different settings in order to plan for appropriate intervention. It allows for all those involved in the process to be engaged with an 'appreciative inquiry' which sets out to create new knowledge, theory and action out of dialogue in order to appreciate individual differences within a wider context (Barrett 2000: 7). This framework can be adapted and used to suit individual children's circumstances.

However, in all circumstances assessment should:

- be embedded in existing knowledge of child development;
- be play-based, functional, ecological and multidimensional;
- follow a certain sequence;
- be undertaken in naturalistic environments;
- identify the child's strengths and emerging skills and competencies as well as problem behaviour;
- identify inhibiting and positive aspects of the environment/ setting where behaviour occurs;
- involve the child and his/her parents to ensure equality of opportunity and non-discriminatory practice;
- be a collaborative process involving family, professionals and other agencies, when it is required;
- involve confidential and unobtrusive practices;

Intervention Action Plan

Name	Date
Problem behaviour/Significant difficulties	Positive behaviour/strengths
Situational/contextual factors–broader factors	
Functions of the behaviour	
Goals and objectives to be achieved	

Form 9.4 An intervention action plan.

- move beyond normative/age-appropriate testing to include criterion-based assessment;
- be evidence-based;
- be viewed as the first step in a potential intervention process.
  (Meisels and Atkins-Burnett 2000; DoH, DfEE and HO 2000; Wilson 1998)

Concluding remarks

Problem behaviour which lasts over a period of time, is frequent and/or severe, should be further assessed to determine its frequency, severity, functions and contextual factors that contribute to it and thus inform the planning of intervention. Assessment is a team approach led by the SENCO or IEP team and actively involves the early years practitioner or teacher, the child and his/ her parents and, where and when necessary, specialists and other professionals with particular expertise. A few cases may be referred for statutory assessment.

Activity 9

- You may like to discuss with a colleague your current system of assessing young children's behaviour problems.
- If you adopt a similar system to that outlined in this chapter, consider what might be the implications for staff and practice in the setting.

Chapter 10

Planning for early intervention

Play-based early intervention

Early intervention is based on the assumption that the early years provide a unique opportunity to (i) influence and enhance children's development, (ii) minimise potential difficulties and the need for special educational services and (iii) enhance the capacity of the families to support children's development (McCollum 2002). Early intervention represents all those efforts made 'to support, facilitate, or alter behaviours' which young children demonstrate (Malone and Langone 1999: 325). In the early years, the use of play as the context in which such efforts take place has led to the notion of play-based intervention (Sigafoos 1999).

Evidence-based early intervention

The use of 'universal panaceas . . . or rigidly applied packages' is now seen to be of little value and their use is considered unwise (Barrett 2000: 7). Wolery (2000) points out that often the same packages and programme are not always appropriate for all children and their families. In addition, in applying these packages educators often tend to focus upon how to replicate them rather than trying to understand their 'underlying driving force' (Visser 2002: 71). Instead, it has now been established that the effectiveness of such evidence-based planning for intervention is beyond dispute (Visser 2002), and assessment provides the evidence required to plan for individualised intervention (McNamara and Hollinger 2003; Pretti-Frontczak et al. 2002; Fox et al. 2002).

There is now little disagreement that the fusion between assessment and intervention is a major change that has taken place over

Behaviour Intervention Plan

Date:

Name:

Duration: From	to	(dates)		

Long-term goals: Reduce fighting with other children

Short-term objectives: Improve social skills & initiate positive interactions

Behaviour management strategies	Environmental modifications	Curriculum modifications	Support and resources required
To use in the early years setting e.g. instructions and guidance, role play and rehearsals, circle time	Reorganise groupings for the child to work with children that can provide support; Direct the child to activities that minimise risk of being involved in fighting	Modify the curriculum to incorporate the identified intervention strategies	Identify cues to remind the child privately of the expected behaviour; Provide positive feedback for expected behaviours displayed; Offer opportunities to rehearse or model expected behaviour; Identify who will be involved with the implementation and monitoring of the programme; Identify possible additional support required and by whom **Family involvement** Discuss with parents the strategies; Involve parents & siblings to follow similar strategies at home
at home e.g. instructions, rehearsals			
Monitoring/recording	State evidence required, when, how often, by whom		
Evaluation	State criteria for the evaluation of the implementation and effectiveness of the behaviour intervention plan		

Form 10.1 A behaviour intervention plan.

recent years in the field of early intervention. The information sum-marised in the 'Intervention Action Plan' forms the basis for the development of an individualised 'Behaviour Intervention Plan' (Lewis 2001) to address the specific needs of an individual child through the existing curriculum and throughout her/his everyday experiences in different settings (early years setting/school, home). According to Kelly and Barnard (2000: 271), 'Assessment is the first step in intervention and should be an ongoing process throughout the intervention.'

Devising a behaviour intervention plan

The Behaviour Intervention Plan is expected to clearly (i) set out long-term goals and short-term objectives, (ii) identify specific intervention strategies to be implemented, (iii) indicate environ-mental and curricular changes and/or modifications needed, (iv) identify support and supplementary resources required, (v) state the duration of the intervention plan, (vi) provide information about the monitoring process and (vii) identify the criteria to be used for the evaluation of the intervention programme (Curtiss *et al.* 2002) (Form 10.1). Ultimately, the Behaviour Intervention Plan should offer a comprehensive programme of support for the devel-opment of appropriate behaviours and the elimination of existing inappropriate behaviours, or clusters of such behaviours.

Long-term goals and short-term objectives

Starting from the goals set out in the Intervention Action Plan, the Behaviour Intervention Plan reiterates long-term goals and identi-fies specific short-term objectives to be achieved. Long-term goals are usually set out on an annual basis and specify the time limit required for them to be achieved. Short-term objectives are the observable and measurable behaviours set out to be reached at regular intervals (e.g. each term) and provide the link between assessing behaviours achieved at those intervals and the behaviour expected to be achieved at the end of the programme (Curtiss *et al.* 2002). For example, for a child who is constantly engaged in fight-ing and for whom a lack of social skills has been assessed as being the underlying factor, short-term objectives may include the improvement of social skills and initiation of positive interactions, whereas a reduction in the rate of fighting remains the long-term goal. Social skills and positive interactions can be defined in observable and measurable behaviours such as using conversational conventions (e.g. please, thank you), turn-taking, non-verbal responses (e.g. smiling, nodding). In cases where short-term objectives are too numerous or the underlying factors are complex or unclear, a judgement should be made to first address behaviours that are most likely to have a knock-on effect on the overall behaviour. Short-term objectives should always remain manageable, otherwise the whole programme may fail to be followed and make a difference for the child.

Behaviour management strategies

Depending on the complexity and severity of the problem behaviour and its function, the behaviour intervention plan may include a single behaviour management strategy or a range of such strategies which form a comprehensive programme of support in both the early years setting and home, if required. In general, behaviour management techniques which support the acquisition or increase of positive behaviours (such as social and problem-solving skills, self-control and self-regulation) should be preferred, while behaviour reduction strategies such as negative reinforcement for inappropriate behaviour should be avoided. If behaviour reduction strategies have been included, these should be gradually phased out as the child develops positive behaviours (Curtiss *et al.* 2002).

Behaviour management strategies should be carefully selected to support the specific behaviours which are the focus of the intervention. Some children's behaviours may need to be addressed by using indirect strategies (for example, modifying the environment), while other children's behaviour may require directed strategies (for example, modelling or role play). Decisions made with regard to whether and when to use non-directed, indirect, guided or directed strategies should be carefully examined so that they meet the individual child's needs (Malone and Langone 1999).

The behaviour intervention plan may also provide a description of the behaviour management strategies and explain which strategies are used for what purpose (e.g. which strategies are used to teach new skills, which to maintain and/or reinforce them) (Curtiss *et al.* 2002). For example, circle time may be used to introduce new skills, praise and rewards may be applied to reinforce the implementation of these skills and role play may be offered as a platform for practising and maintaining the new skills. Davis *et al.* (2004) point out that a combination of approaches and strategies are more effective in facilitating positive behaviour and eliminating problem behaviour than a single approach.

In general, behaviour management techniques should build upon the child's strengths and competencies and be embedded into her/his experiences, whereas, at the same time, they aim to expand the child's experience (Curtiss *et al.* 2002; Quinn *et al.* 1998). For instance, for a child with good language and communication skills, guidance and instructions may be used as part of a social skills training programme to introduce social skills and positive interactions. For a child with limited language and communication skills, modelling may precede guidance and instructions, which, in turn, may introduce new, and expand existing, language and communication skills. These skills may be further supported through expressive arts and emotional literacy (e.g. role play and rehearsals) and circle time which offer opportunity for practice, whereas the systematic and consistent use of mutually agreed discrete cues (such as nodding, smiling, gestures etc) and praise and rewards may be used to provide extrinsic motivation for the child to participate in the programme (Quinn *et al.* 1998).

Changes and modifications in the learning environment

Intervention programmes cannot be successful if changes focus only on the individual child. Important changes in the environment must also be made to enhance the child's existing competencies and protect the child from potential events that increase problem behaviour (Brown *et al.* 2002; Sameroff and Fiese 2000). The behaviour management strategies adopted may also require systematic changes, adjustments and modifications in the environment of the setting (e.g. routines and schedules, grouping of children and seating arrangements, rearranging furniture, bringing in or removing resources etc) (Curtiss *et al.* 2002). For instance, if fighting takes place in particular places or activities, then systematically adding or removing resources or regulating the number of children involved in the play and learning activities may be some possible changes to be considered. If the same children are always involved in fighting, then systematically regrouping children or providing clear guidance and instructions may bring about changes in behaviour.

Curriculum modifications and changes

Behaviour management strategies should also be carefully chosen and planned so that they are interlinked and easily incorporated into the existing early years curricula. In this way, the child is enabled to access a coherent and meaningful programme of support rather than having partial and unrelated input offered by individual behaviour management strategies implemented out of context (Gimpell and Holland 2003). In addition, incorporating and implementing behaviour management through the existing curriculum minimises disruption to existing structures (Curtiss *et al*. 2002). Adhering to an inclusive ethos, behaviour management techniques should take place within existing early years programmes, although the provision made for the individual child may be different or additional to that offered to all children. Depending on the hypothesis concerning the functions of the behaviour, often modifications in the learning environment, the content and mode of delivery of the curriculum may prove enough to eliminate some problem behaviours (Quinn *et al*. 1998).

Support and resources required

For Behaviour Intervention Plans to be implemented, as designed, early years settings/schools should be prepared to commit time and resources (Lewis 2001). Therefore, staff, time and, if relevant, training required should be clearly identified in the Behaviour Intervention Plan (Curtiss *et al*. 2002; Quinn *et al*. 1998). For instance, to facilitate the development of certain social skills in identified activities may require that the Learning Support Assistant is deployed to (i) work closely with the child and facilitate her/his participation in the activities and (ii) to observe and keep a record of whether the activities have been implemented as they were initially planned, and the level of the child's participation in them. Usually the demands made upon the time of staff and their training needs receive little attention in the development of Behaviour Intervention Plans. However, these elements have been found to be decisive factors in the successful implementation and effectiveness of behaviour intervention plans (Reimers *et al*. 1987). Staff then should be allocated time and undertake training required to fulfil these commitments.

It must also be noted here that although most problem behaviours can, and must, be addressed via existing early years programmes, some behaviours, due to the severity and intensity which they present, may require specialist interventions provided by the school counsellor, school psychologist and speech and language therapist and, in some cases, even from the medical profession (Quinn *et al.* 1998).

Family involvement

Comprehensive Behaviour Intervention Plans need to go beyond the input offered at the early years setting and make provision about the management of the behaviour at home. Ulrich and Bauer (2003) point out that parents might be surprised to hear that their child experiences problems, but they will be shocked to find out that the early years setting or school has identified such problems without informing them. Therefore, communication with parents at the very early stages is very important (Wilson 2001).

Parents are the most significant and influential resource for young children and they have important information and insights to contribute to the process of planning and implementing a Behaviour Intervention Plan (Fox and Dunlop 2002). They should be consulted and participate in discussions to (i) voice their expectations and determine the goals of the programme, (ii) indicate and agree on the ways they can be involved and support the implementation of the programme at home, (iii) indicate how they themselves need to be supported and (iv) collect and provide information for the evaluation of the programme (Fox and Dunlop 2002).

Behaviour Intervention Plans developed in partnership with the family can have at least a threefold outcome. First, they offer continuity and consistent application of the behaviour management programme across the early years settings and the family. For example, if behaviours which are reinforced in the early years setting are also reinforced at home, and/or behaviours which are ignored in the early years setting are also ignored at home, then the child receives consistent messages that reinforce appropriate behaviour, while contributing to the elimination of inappropriate behaviour. In contrast, inconsistent practices within and between the two systems may become confusing in the eyes of the child and contribute to the deterioration of the child's behaviour.

Second, they provide opportunities and support for the family to develop new skills and ways of interacting with the child and third, contribute to changes in the family system as a result of the child's improved behaviour (Fox and Dunlop 2002). Consistent application of behaviour management techniques may require that parents (and family members) receive support to acquire a good understanding of the techniques and the necessary skills to implement them. The more confident parents are in dealing with children's behaviour the more successful the intervention programmes (Linfoot *et al.* 1999). In interactional terms, often change in parental behaviour itself alters the dynamics and patterns of interactions within the family that, in turn, influence the child's behaviour which again impacts on the family relationships.

Behaviour management strategies should not only be negotiated and agreed by parents, but they should also be based on the assessment of the family's strengths and needs in order to achieve effective collaboration (Beverly and Thomas 1999). The family's circumstances, pressures and parents' work and other family commitments should be taken into account to develop behaviour strategies that are not too complex or burdensome and offer coaching and support in developing the required skills. Programmes that do not present additional pressures to the family and are easily understood and implemented are more likely to be applied as initially intended than are programmes which are too complicated and demanding (Fox and Dunlop 2002). Support planned for parents should be provided by informal face-to-face meetings, print materials and videos rather than in formal ways by professionals and organisations with formal structures and procedures (Linfoot *et al.* 1999).

Monitoring and evaluating Behaviour Intervention Plans

The implementation of Behaviour Intervention Plans is expected to be systematically monitored and evaluated to determine (i) the extent to which the goals and objectives set out have been achieved (that is, effectiveness) and (ii) the degree to which individual intervention strategies and the behaviour intervention plan as a whole have been systematically and consistently applied during the specified period (that is, successful implementation) (Curtiss *et al.* 2002; Quinn *et al.* 1998; Bryer 1988).

The monitoring and evaluation of a Behaviour Intervention Plan requires a scientific methodology that provides appropriate evidence for making judgements about its effective and successful implementation (Carr cited in Fox *et al.* 2002; Pretti-Frontczak *et al.* 2002). However, although there is now much awareness and training in assessing children's needs and developing individualised Behaviour Intervention Plans, the monitoring and evaluation of these plans have received little attention. Often Behaviour Intervention Plans fail to demonstrate their successful implementation and their effectiveness either because no monitoring system has been identified or because outcomes have not been defined in observable and measurable terms.

Devising a monitoring system

A Behaviour Intervention Plan should clearly identify (i) a schedule for both ongoing and summative data collection, (ii) the measures to be used (observations, checklist, interviews) and (iii) the person responsible for data collection (early years setting/class teacher, teacher assistant etc) (Curtiss *et al.* 2002; Horner *et al.* 2001). Ongoing data collection usually takes place through informal observations throughout the implementation of the Behaviour Intervention Plan or in specified periods of time (e.g. each term) through the use of systematic observations or checklists to evaluate short-term objectives. Summative data is collected at the end of the implementation of the Behaviour Intervention Plan to evaluate its overall outcomes. To have comparable data, summative data collection requires that the same tools used to collect baseline data during initial assessment are used again at the end of the programme.

Early years practitioners are well acquainted with the High/ Scope 'Plan–Do–Review' approach which provides an appropriate structure for the development of a monitoring and evaluation system (Barrett 2000) (Figure 10.1). Following the same procedures used in the High/Scope approach, early years practitioners can develop a monitoring system that provides the evidence required to evaluate the successful implementation and effectiveness of each component (that is, each behaviour management strategy) and the Behaviour Intervention Plan as a whole.

Figure 10.1 A 'Plan–Do–Review' approach to behaviour intervention.

Record keeping

A monitoring system is as good as its recording system. A good recording system should provide accurate, factual and measurable information with regard to (i) the way the behaviour management strategies are implemented (e.g. their consistent and regular employment, demands made on time and staff that cannot be met, skills and competencies not available, disruption in the programme, any unforeseen circumstances etc) and (ii) the child's response to behaviour management techniques (e.g. acquisition of new behaviours and changes in or elimination of inappropriate behaviour).

In general, a good recording system should strive for simplicity and efficiency by minimising the amount of time required to learn the system and to gather, summarise and use the information for decision making (Horner *et al.* 2001). It is important to note here that any recording system developed should aim not only to collect data for accountability purposes, but also to aid thinking and inform the decision-making process (Horner *et al.* 2001; Bryer 1988). Therefore, the decision about the kind of data to be collected, when, how often and by whom should be issues for careful consideration.

Identifying the criteria for evaluation

For ongoing and summative evaluation, it is important to identify the criteria that will be taken into account to make judgements about the effectiveness and successful implementation of a Behaviour Intervention Plan (Curtiss *et al.* 2002). The short-term objectives of the intervention programme, broken down into small observable and measurable elements of behaviour, can form the criteria for ongoing evaluation. For example, social skills intended to be achieved may include a range of conversational conventions (using appropriate language), interpretation of and response to non-verbal cues (making eye contact, smiling etc), turn-taking, initiating interactions etc. The overall goals set out for the Behaviour Intervention Plan are the focus of summative evaluation. Whether these goals have been achieved or not will be decided from the data collected at the end of the programme by using the same instruments which have been used for screening and assessment (checklists, observations and interviews with parents and the children themselves).

The fusion between assessment and intervention

Assessment and intervention (planning, monitoring and evaluation) are closely interlinked and form an ongoing continuous process that might be repeated as necessary (Figure 10.2). If the ongoing evaluation demonstrates that the intended short-term objectives and long-term goals have been achieved, the programme may cease. If progress has been made but not all objectives have been achieved, the intervention programme may continue and/or be modified if evidence suggests so. If no progress has been made, then the child's needs should be reassessed and on the basis of the new information a modified or new intervention plan may be devised. According to Meisels and Atkins-Burnett (2000) the development and implementation of Behaviour Intervention Plans should test the initial hypotheses and/or lead to new hypotheses. Assessment and intervention form ongoing interactive processes that inform each other.

Meisels and Atkins-Burnett (2000: 249–50) argue that there is a fusion between assessment and intervention on the grounds of three fundamental assumptions:

> The first assumption is that assessment is a dynamic enterprise that calls on information from multiple sources collected throughout numerous time points reflecting a wide range of child experiences and caregiver interpretations. The second assumption is that the formal act of assessment is only the first step in the process of acquiring information about the child and family. Through intervention – by putting into practice the ideas or hypotheses raised by the initial assessment procedures – more information will be acquired that can serve

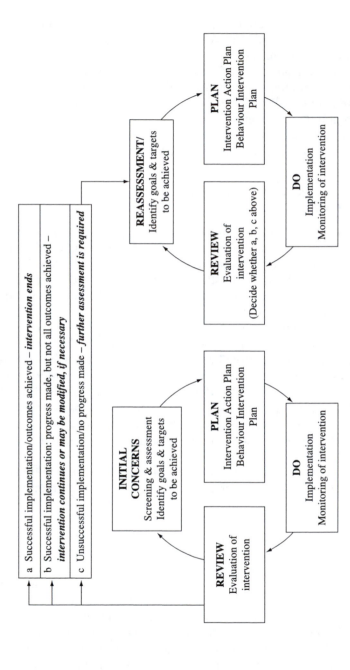

Figure 10.2 A continuous, ongoing evidence-based process for problem behaviour assessment, intervention planning, monitoring and evaluation.

the dual purpose of refining the assessment and enhancing the intervention. Third, assessment is of limited value in the absence of intervention. The meaning of assessment is closely tied to its utility, which is its contribution to decision making about practice or intervention or its confirmation of a child's continuing progress.

Factors influencing Behaviour Intervention Plans

The successful implementation of a Behaviour Intervention Plan depends on factors such as good understanding and its acceptability for those who are called on to implement it (e.g. the early years practitioner/teacher, Learning Support Assistant), its effectiveness and the level of disruption caused, and demands which are made upon resources and staff (Schneider et al. 1992; Wood 1991; Peck et al. 1989; Webster 1989; Reimers et al. 1987) (Figure 10.3). If the intervention strategies and the programme are not understood well, then it is more likely not to be implemented consistently with the result of not bringing about the expected outcomes. If there is a good understanding, but the intervention strategies or the programme are not considered suitable or acceptable, again there is a danger of them not being applied as they were initially designed, and therefore the outcomes once again may not be achieved. If the programme is understood well and it is acceptable, but its effectiveness is limited, it is more likely to be abandoned as the outcomes may not materialise. Finally, although a programme may be well understood, is acceptable and effective, if it causes a great deal of disruption in the setting because of its complexity and demands on resources, again it may not be implemented systematically, with the result that the objectives set out in the intervention plan are not achieved. In general, behaviour management strategies that are the least intrusive with respect to existing structures are usually preferred and consistently used (Curtiss et al. 2002; Witt and Martens 1983).

In addition to these variables, Visser (2002) argues that there are 'eternal verities' that underline any approach used to deal with behaviour problems. These include empathy and equity, building positive relationships and using humour, transparent communications, setting up boundaries and challenges, planning for instructional reactions (acknowledging the cause-and-effect relationship of behaviours), believing that behaviours can change

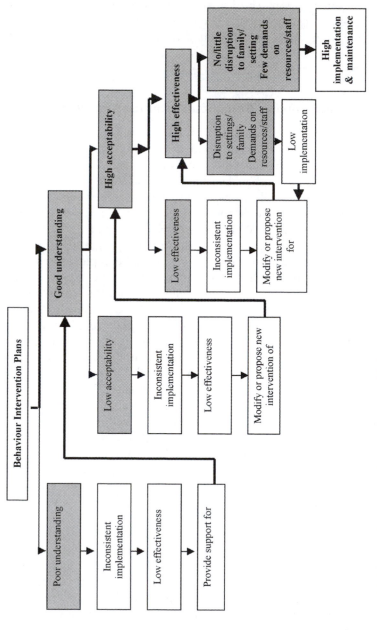

Figure 10.3 Factors affecting the implementation of Behaviour Intervention Plans (adapted from Reimers et al. 1987).

and emotional needs can be met and that preventative measures are better than intervention (Visser 2002). Eternal verities, according to Visser (2002: 74), are 'truths that are apparent in the web and weave of approaches. They are eternal in as much as they are necessary to the proficiency of all approaches regardless of the timeframe in which approaches are being developed and applied.' Visser argues that in constantly seeking 'new' solutions, educators have lost sight of the essential factors that make interventions work.

Behaviour Intervention Plans: whose responsibility?

The development of Behaviour Intervention Plans is mainly the responsibility of the SENCO or IEP Team; however, the early years practitioner/teacher, who has the direct responsibility for the child and, ultimately, is the one who will implement the programme, should always be directly involved in the process. S/he can provide curriculum information and information with regard to changes or modifications needed in the environment and voice her/his expectations (Quinn et al. 1998). The early years practitioner and all paraeducators (such as Learning Support Assistant, key worker etc) should also ensure that they have a good understanding of the Behaviour Intervention Plan, and raise any concerns regarding its acceptability and effectiveness as well as the demands made upon their time and resources. A Behaviour Intervention Plan involves the systematic, structured and team-based planning and implementation of behaviour management. A Behaviour Intervention Plan is not just a management tool devised in response to legal requirements and for accountability purposes only. Instead, it is a proactive tool for developing a repertoire of positive behaviours to counteract problem behaviour (Curtiss et al. 2002).

Concluding remarks

Planning for early intervention requires that all information collected during assessment is taken into account to create a Behaviour Intervention Plan which counteracts the factors which contribute to or are associated with the identified problem behaviour. Early intervention which is evidence-based and is easily incorporated in existing curricula serves the needs of individual children better than the replication of any 'panaceas' deemed to be effective. A system for monitoring and evaluating behaviour intervention plans is just as important as its planning.

 Activity 10

> You may like to review Behaviour Intervention Plans which you currently use:
>
> • to examine the extent to which they are based on the evidence provided through assessment;
> • to consider, if necessary, any changes to their format in the light of the information provided in this chapter.

Chapter 11

Traits, knowledge, skills and competencies

Behaviour management and personal and professional competencies

In the mid-1980s, Chazan and Laing (1985) highlighted that in educational settings, teachers often appear unwilling to deal with children's behaviour problems, suggesting that either it is not their job or the source of the problem is outside of the school and they can do nothing about it or, in the case of young children, problem behaviours will pass with time. A number of authors have argued that teachers should not be criticised for holding such views, since the nature and source of problem behaviours are complex and teachers often do not have the same level of training as specialists such as psychologists, social workers and therapists (Douglas 1989; Galloway and Goodwin 1987; Chazan and Laing 1985; Jenkins *et al.* 1984; Laing 1984; Davie *et al.* 1972). However, in dealing with large groups of children in a class or early years setting, the reality is that (i) habitual preventative behaviour management is a basic part of the duties of teachers and early years practitioners and (ii) behaviour problems increasingly raise concerns, and existing policies and regulations require that schools and early years settings have in place appropriate structures and appropriately trained and equipped staff for early intervention.

Research, literature and common experience have shown that authority over children, behaviour control, externally imposed discipline and punitive approaches are not effective in changing behaviour in the long term, although children may be contained or controlled within the particular setting. Many authors argue that how behaviour management is approached, at either habitual and preventative level and/or early intervention level, depends on the practitioner's own personal traits and characteristics, knowledge, skills and competencies (Visser 2002; Weiss 2002a, b; Zabel 1988b; Roberts 1983; Docking 1980).

Traits and personal characteristics

Teachers' and early years practitioners' own traits and characteristics are influential in determining the way problem behaviours are dealt with, and one important variable is an empathetic understanding. Empathy requires teachers to adjust their ideas and see things from the child's point of view (Cooper 1990). Being empathetic does not mean excusing the child's behaviour, but rather continuously asking 'Why do I think this child behaved in this way and what does it mean for the approach I use?' (Visser 2002: 78). Problem behaviours often serve some kind of function for the child who may often behave as s/he does in order to get something or avoid something and, in the case of young children, because of not fully developed skills and competencies (Foster-Johnson and Dunlop 1993).

Traits such as warmth, patience, caring, a sense of humour and respect for children are also important contributory factors in dealing effectively with behaviour problems (Visser 2002; Zabel 1988b). It is suggested that many difficulties, particularly with young children, ease if treated with warmth and patience, while 'a sense of humour', carefully and respectfully used (not teasing or laughing at), may help children to see the funny side of their own unintentionally amusing behaviour (Roberts 1983). Teachers' and early years practitioners' respect shows children that they are treated seriously as significant persons (Docking 1980). In addition, respectful teachers and early years practitioners are respected, in return, and win the collaboration and good will of children (Ellis *et al.* 2003).

Furthermore, teachers' awareness of their own perceptions and interpretations of children's behaviour problems and the way they choose to deal, or not deal, with them is an influential factor in the elimination or continuation of at least some of children's problem behaviours (Brophy and Rohrkember 1981). Weiss (2002a) places particular emphasis on the way teachers' and early years practitioners' awareness of their own personal past experiences may unconsciously colour their interpretation of children's behaviour and the formation of interpersonal relationships. He states that 'past interpersonal experiences form a template that shapes and may distort teachers' views of present situations. Teachers are often unaware of their personal subjective involvement in what they consider to be objective professional decisions about children' (Weiss 2002b: 122). Early experiences are often buried in individuals' unconscious states of mind and may result in 'collateral outcomes', either positive or negative (Ballard 1991). Weiss (2002b: 114), quoting Arthur Jersild, points out that children are better served 'when teachers face themselves'.

Teachers are only a part of other less immediately evident variables that play a role in behaviour management. Pupils themselves are far from passive entities and their own personal characteristics, skills and overall performance and even their family's background and circumstances are important factors in how their behaviour is perceived and/or managed (Safran *et al.* 1990; Roberts 1983). Weiss (2002b: 122) exemplifies this by stating that 'A child's skills, abilities or interests may elicit particular feelings. A child's age, gender, body build, height, skin color or other physical characteristics can stimulate recollections of the teacher's own childhood self-image and self-concept.' He goes on to state that these characteristics may cause teachers and early years professionals either to 'fall in love' or 'fall in hate', pointing out that 'To psychologically "fall in love" with a child, where the idealized youngster can do no wrong, may be as destructive as "falling in hate", where the devalued child can do no right' (Weiss 2002b: 122).

Early years practitioners' and teachers' ability to seek, and have access to, children's views on how they experience events and situations is another variable that influences behaviour management. Ability and skills to explore, for instance, 'everyday life events' allow early years practitioners to gain a better understanding of individual children's needs and make appropriate arrangements that best serve their needs. Often the needs of children for 'belongingness and a sense of place in the classroom' are dismissed or forgotten and if they then become the focus of reprimands may deeply frustrate children and intensify problem behaviours (Ellis *et al.* 2003: 6).

Communication then becomes an important skill for developing relationships that allow access into children's thinking and world. Wheatley (1992: 38) argues that there is a need for all professionals to develop 'better skills in listening, communicating and facilitating groups, because these are the talents that build strong relationships'. Awareness of group dynamics and the way they influence relationships is also an important factor as it may facilitate or inhibit interaction that leads to positive behaviour.

While traits and personal characteristics are part of individuals' personality and predispositions, it does not mean that they cannot be transformed or altered. An understanding of the way personal characteristics and traits influence the interpretation of social circumstances and the interrelationships created, and systematic reflection on their own traits and characteristics, may allow professionals to achieve a state of personal awareness that does justice to their role and the way they serve children.

Knowledge, skills and competencies

Early years practitioners' and teachers' knowledge of and skills in dealing with behaviour problems are also important factors in dealing with problem behaviours. Problem behaviours, being context-specific phenomena (Denscombe 1985), require that the overall context of the classroom or early years setting needs to be carefully reviewed in a systematic and purposeful manner in order to create possibilities for preventative behaviour management strategies and programmes (Morgan and Dunn 1990; Roberts 1983). Indeed, such knowledge and skills are often found to form part of teacher preparation programmes that address such skills as 'Managing and organizing the classroom . . . planning rules and procedures . . . making clear the consequences and rewards for appropriate and inappropriate behaviour . . . providing time for explanation, rehearsal, and feedback' (Zabel 1988b: 174).

In addition to this, certain skills and competencies specific to early identification of, and early intervention for, problem behaviours are required in order effectively to address children's needs in educational settings. These include (i) knowledge and understanding of young children's psychological growth and development, (ii) knowledge and understanding of behaviour problems, (iii) skills and competencies in screening and assessment and ability to interpret findings, (iv) skills and competencies in planning for intervention, (v) knowledge and ability to make appropriate use of existing resources; knowledge of group work, in order to develop a whole-school approach, (vi) understanding of culture diversity and class differences, and the problems arising because of socio-economic disadvantage and circumstances creating tension and hostility, (vii) ability to develop whole school/early years setting approaches, (viii) ability to work with parents collaboratively, (ix) knowledge of competencies and roles of related professions and (x) knowledge of community organisations, resources and other outside agencies and ability to work with them (Killoran *et al.* 2001; Falconer-Hall and Harlatt 1989; Zabel 1988b):

The basic skills and competencies to be achieved have been tentatively summarised on Form 11.1 for professionals' own self-assessment. This form can be used by professionals who work with young children in different capacities (e.g. nursery teacher, Learning Support Assistant, SENCO, IEP team member etc) to self-assess their existing skills and competencies as well as their learning needs for staff development. Five levels of mastery, as these have been defined by Killoran *et al.* (2001), can be used by practitioners and professionals to identify the level of mastery of their existing skills and competencies. The five levels of mastery are: *unfamiliar* which shows little or no information on this skill or competency; *awareness* which shows that the skill and competency is familiar, but more training is required; *knowledge* where one can speak knowledgeably about the topic, but support and further training are required; *application* which shows that the skill can be used in a variety of situations in a satisfactory level; and *mastery* where the skill can be used independently in a variety of situations and its use is understood at an exemplary level. Considering the range of professionals working with young children, application and mastery need to be demonstrated by professionals and practitioners with appropriate training (nursery teacher, early years teacher, qualified early years practitioner) or specialists (SENCO, IEP team members), whereas awareness and knowledge need to be demonstrated by paraprofessionals (variously named as paraeducators, Learning Support Assistants, teacher assistants, lay helpers).

The involvement of paraprofessionals

Currently, particular emphasis has been placed on the role and training of paraprofessionals in early intervention programmes. Paraprofessionals are individuals who have not received professional training by following traditional routes of undergraduate or

Self-assessment of personal and professional knowledge, skills and competencies

State your role *:

Date

Knowledge, traits, skills and competencies	Level of mastery **				
	Unfamiliar	Awareness	Knowledge	Application	Mastery
Personal and interpersonal skills					
Self-awareness of own attitudes, values and biases					
Showing empathy, understanding and acceptance					
Knowledge of own limitations					
Ability to ask for help and support					
Effective communication					
Positive social interactions					
Awareness of group/team dynamics					
Ability to address differences in opinion and arguments					
Child knowledge					
Child development/Factors associated with development					
Behaviour problems, screening and assessment issues					
Terminology and definition of behaviour problems					
Functions of screening					
Screening process					
Functions of assessment					
Assessment process					
Observation skills					
Selection and administration of assessment tools					
Interviewing skills					
Awareness of confidentiality issues and ability to deal with ethical dilemmas					
Working with families					
Impact of behaviour problems on family					

Respect of family's culture, values and diversity						
Sharing information with, and involving, the family						
Partnership with families						
Assisting family to engage in assessment & intervention						
Assisting families in accessing information and services						
Advocating for families						
Planning for intervention						
Setting up intervention goals and objectives						
Designing assessment-based intervention						
Integrating intervention within daily programme						
Monitoring and evaluation of intervention						
Adaptation of intervention programme						
Designing problem-solving interventions						
Creating appropriate environments						
Implementation of intervention						
Service coordination						
Relevant law, regulations and requirements						
Existing statutory, non-governmental and voluntary services						
Working in partnership with other agencies						

Form 11.1 A self-assessment checklist for personal and professional traits, knowledge, skills and competencies (adapted from Killoran et al. 2001).

* State your role: e.g. nursery teacher, teacher assistant, SENCO, IEP team member etc.

** Levels of mastery: Unfamiliar, Awareness, Knowledge, Application, Mastery.

postgraduate training (Musick and Stott 2000). They usually provide direct service to children and their families under the supervision of teachers or other professionals (Killoran *et al.* 2001).

In general, the effective use of paraprofessionals depends on wise recruitment and provision of well conceived and implemented training and supervision integrated into the goals of the programme (Musick and Stott 2000). Specific competencies identified as being a priority for paraprofessionals' training needs are (i) child development and disability, (ii) family involvement, (iii) service delivery (e.g. knowledge of early childhood best practice, ability to create appropriate environments, ability to communicate effectively with children, ability to integrate therapeutic practices into learning environments, ability to monitor child progress and make changes in the programme, ability to adapt programmes), (iv) programme management (e.g. knowledge of programme vision, goals, guidelines and operating procedures) and (v) professional development, ethics (Killoran *et al.* 2001).

The development and establishment of a working relationship between paraprofessionals and teachers/early years professionals is a factor that affects greatly the way the children are served. Consistent communication is a necessity for the immediate resolution of conflicting views which may surround critical and uncomfortable events. Often, seeing things from a different perspective alleviates differences, and humour tactfully and respectfully applied may become a catalyst in uncomfortable situations (Zabolio McGrath 2002).

A whole school/early years setting approach

Early years practitioners and teachers are often the first interface between parents and their children's 'out of home' professional care and they have a responsibility to encourage mutuality in the shared process of the education and care of children. Coleman (1998: 155–6) argues that to serve the children best and meet their needs adequately, educational settings should go beyond techniques or practices which are narrowly defined around curricular demands, to embrace broader responsibilities and develop systems of support that operate at different levels of functioning. Safran and Oswald (2003) state that schools and, for young children, early years settings need to have structures and policies which allow for supporting (i) individual children who exhibit persistent and severe problems, (ii) groups of pupils or clusters of behaviours (e.g. bullying, aggression) frequently observed among children, (iii) behaviours exhibited outside the classroom (e.g. playground, communal areas) and (iv) prevention of problem behaviours.

This kind of support requires a whole school/early years setting approach for positive behaviour support which is characterised by (i) collective goals attained by providing appropriate support at different levels, (ii) monitoring the collective goals set out to be achieved, (iii) sharing information and developing skills to analyse and interpret information and (iv) staff development which emphasises research skills necessary for the development of evidence-based practice (Safran and Oswald 2003; Coleman 1998). These systems of support require mechanisms for facilitating collaboration at different levels, that is, within the educational setting, with parents and with other service providers and agencies (Anderson and Matthews 2001). The notion of developing systems of support and care emphasises the importance of whole school approaches as well as communication and collaboration with families and other agencies.

Partnership and collaboration with family

Coleman (1998: 151) states that collaborative teachers believe that when parents are brought into the relationship, it makes education 'easier . . . for the kid, the parent, and the teacher'. In addition, a strong relationship with parents encourages continuity for the child, good communication, participation and ownership. Coleman (1998) highlights the importance of adopting a cooperative learning model which provides for both groups (that is, parents and professionals) goals and individual accountability. This requires caring relationships which are characterised by mutual responsiveness and respectfulness rather than imbalance in status and power (Sumsion 1999).

Borrowing from Turnbull et al. (2000) and Meggitt (1997), the evolution of relationships between parents and professionals is represented in Figure 11.1. Up to the 1960s, when the medical paradigm dominated the field, professionals were seen as the experts who had the ultimate responsibility for decision making. In the 1970s, with the behavioural model gaining credence, parents were seen as a resource and received training to support their

Models of professionals' and parents' relationships

The expert model (up to the 1960s)

Parents
as passive recipients

Professionals
as experts;
in full control of
decision making

Skills transmission model (in the 1970s)

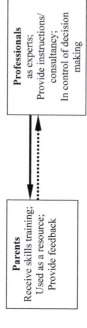

Parents
Receive skills training;
Used as a resource;
Provide feedback

Professionals
as experts;
Provide instructions/
consultancy;
In control of decision
making

The collaborative or family-centred model (in the 1980s)

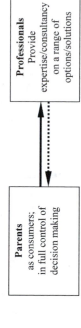

Parents
as consumers;
in full control of
decision making

Professionals
Provide
expertise/consultancy
on a range of
options/solutions

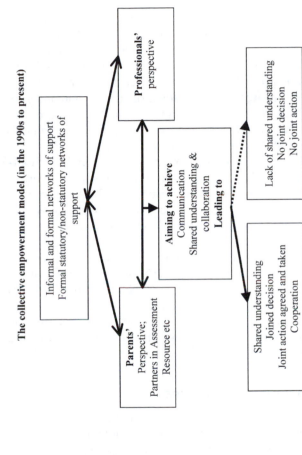

The collective empowerment model (in the 1990s to present)

Informal and formal networks of support
Formal statutory/non-statutory networks of support

Professionals' perspective

Parents' Perspective; Partners in Assessment Resource etc

Aiming to achieve Communication Shared understanding & collaboration **Leading to**

Shared understanding Joined decision Joint action agreed and taken Cooperation

Lack of shared understanding No joint decision No joint action

Resolution of disagreement

Figure 11.1 Different models of parent–professional relationships (after Turnbull *et al.* 2000; Meggitt 1997).

children, yet the professionals still remained the experts and decision makers. By the 1980s, with the influence of the inter-actionist and systemic theories, the balance in the equation changed. Although professionals still remained the experts, parents became consumers who received facts and information to ulti-mately make an informed decision.

Turnbull *et al.* (2000: 641), drawing from the work of many researchers, state that 'the contemporary focus is collective empowerment, in which all participants (i.e. professionals and families) increase their capacity and mastery over the resources needed to achieve mutually desired outcomes'. Both parents and professionals are supported by existing statutory, formal and infor-mal networks of support to assist each other and become collec-tively empowered in order to work towards agreed outcomes for the child (Turnbull *et al.* 2000; Meggitt 1997). While, currently, emphasis is placed on collective empowerment, the other models of partnership are still evident in existing practice.

Comprehensive systems of support require (i) regular school–home and home–school communication, preferably in an informal manner for professionals and parents to share their experiences and stories (Sumsion 1999), (ii) help for families (e.g. assessment of family needs, organised, coordinated activities to address such needs) and support so that identified strategies and programmes are consistently implemented across family and early years settings and (iii) parental collaboration with schools and links with a network of community service resources (health centres, GPs etc) for shared programmes (McAllister Swap 1993). While collective empowerment is the current focus, the expert, skills transmission and collaborative models are still evident in professionals' and parents' relationships.

Collaboration with other services

Although teachers and early years professionals usually tend to deal with the majority of problems within the school by making use of educational resources, they often need the support of specialist services, especially for children who show persistent and severe problems (Ford and Nikapota 2000). In addition, the fact that early years practitioners and teachers are often working with highly vulnerable families facing distinct challenges, and parents who are preoccupied with issues other than the needs of their children, may make it necessary to seek and make use of community-based services which offer resources and specialist expertise (Halpern 2000). Indeed, there is currently much discussion about collaboration among service providers and the provision of comprehensive and continuous, seamless services (Halpern 2000).

Collaboration with other services means that the assessment of, and planning for, problem behaviour becomes a joint responsibility of professionals who have different expertise and can provide services, when necessary, that go beyond the individual child within the educational setting but also at home and in the community (Talay-Ongan 2001). Although early years practitioners and teachers may feel overwhelmed by participating in service collaboration, the benefits far outweigh initial challenges. In addition, their knowledge of children and their needs and their knowledge of the type of care and education offered in the setting are likely to be respected and given due attention in service collaboration teams (Demers and Gudgeon 2004). In a way, service collaboration is incomplete without the involvement of educators (Anderson and Matthews 2001).

However, it must be noted here that service collaboration and coordination is far from easy. Research studies on interprofessional working are proliferating and the difficulties of bringing together services which have different roles and responsibilities and priorities are well documented. The development of a common language and framework for communication and service collaboration may be emerging, but is not yet a reality (Ford and Nikapota 2000).

Training and professional development

The overview of early years practitioners' and teachers' traits, knowledge, skills and competencies shows that they can make a considerable difference in the way problem behaviours are dealt with. Indeed, educators dealing with children's behaviour problems do use many of these competencies (Lidz 1983). They do try to understand the functions behaviours serve for children at particular developmental stages (Foster-Johnson and Dunlap 1993), explain behaviour problems in terms of children's gender and differences in cultural background and manipulate the environment and plan rewards and consequences (Dadson and Horner 1993). In addition, they are expected to and do cooperate with parents (Panter 1992; Jones *et al.* 1989), colleagues and other professionals (O'Hagan and Smith 1993; David 1989).

It seems, however, that the application of these skills and competencies is often arbitrary and lacks systematic proactive planning and monitoring that is placed on sound conceptual frameworks. Researchers argue that behaviour management needs a conceptual and skills-based approach (Martin and Norwich 1991; Zabel 1988b) which incorporates (i) teachers' common-sense knowledge being interrogated in the light of relevant philosophical and conceptual frameworks and (ii) skills for evidence-based practice which allow them to test and generate hypotheses concerning potentially effective interventions and develop techniques that are appropriate for individual children (Visser 2002; Shea and Bauer 1987; Denscombe 1985).

This view is further supported by Burden (1992: 43) who claims that 'Pragmatic approaches to fostering "good" behaviour in educational settings are of limited value if they are not contextualized within a coherent theory of teaching and learning.' These observations lend support to the argument that early years professionals and teachers should place emphasis on continuing professional development that focuses on learning rather than teaching (Powis 2002). That means that early years professionals, instead of being taught strategies and techniques and panaceas deemed to be appropriate for dealing with behaviour problems, need to learn to have a critical understanding of young children's behaviour problems and the processes of early identification and behaviour management. As Professor Weiss (2003) claims, 'a good teacher is a good learner' and this book has aimed to support such learning.

Concluding remarks

The complexity of human nature, the unpredictability of children's reactions to particular settings which they inhabit, and the multi-faceted relationships existing in an ecosystem such as that of the early years setting classroom require an early years practitioner teacher who has a strong knowledge base, has specific skills and competencies, is proactive rather than reactive and is alert and observant and guided intuitively and knowledgeably to handle behaviour problems by showing understanding, empathy, patience, warmth and a sense of humour. Effective and successful behaviour management requires a multi-skilled and competent early years professional/teacher whose practice is informed by, and based on, evidence which is examined and interrogated in the light of existing theoretical and conceptual frameworks.

Activity 11

- Using the self-assessment form, you may like to identify your existing skills and competencies and training needs according to your role and responsibilities in the early years setting.
- Using the different models of parental professional partnership, you may like to have discussions with colleagues to identify the model which reflects best your current practice.

References

Achenbach, T.M. and Edelbrock, C.S. (1978) 'The classification of child psychopathology: a review and analysis of empirical attempts', *Psychological Bulletin*, Vol. 85, pp. 1275–301.

Achenbach, T.M. and Edelbrock, C.S. (1983) 'Taxonomic issues in child psychopathology', in T.H. Ollendick and M. Hersen (eds) *Handbook of Child Psychopathology*, New York: Pergamon.

Achenbach, T.M. and McConaughy, S.H. (1987) *Empirically Based Assessment of Child and Adolescent Psychopathology. Practical Applications*, Newbury Park, CA: Sage.

Ahmad, A. and Bano, M. (1996) 'Effective behaviour guidance in schools', *Proceedings of the BPS*, Vol. 4, No. 1, p. 13.

Aiello, J.R., Nicosia, G. and Thompson, D.E. (1979) 'Physiological, social and behavioral consequences of crowding on children and adolescents', *Child Development*, Vol. 50, pp. 195–202.

Algozzine, B. (1980) 'The disturbing child: a matter of opinion', *Behavioral Disorders*, Vol. 5, No. 2, pp. 112–15.

Alimisi, (1988) 'The social perspective of the problem of absenteeism of pupils from the 9-year compulsory education' (in Greek), *Ta Ekpaideftika*, Vol. 13, pp. 124–33.

Allport, G.W. (1973) 'Attitudes in the history of social psychology', in N. Warren and M. Jahoda (eds) *Attitudes*, Harmondsworth: Penguin Books.

Anderson, J.A. and Matthews, B. (2001) 'We care . . . for students with emotional and behavioral disabilities and their families', *TEACHING Exceptional Children*, Vol. 33, No. 5, pp. 34–9.

APA (1987) *Quick Reference to the Diagnostic Criteria from DSM-III-R*, Arlington, VA: American Psychiatric Association.

Arthur, M., Bochner, S. and Butterfield, N. (1999) 'Enhancing peer interactions within the context of play', *International Journal of Disability, Development and Education*, Vol. 46, No. 3, pp. 367–81.

Atwater, J.B. and Morris, E.K. (1988) 'Teachers' instructions and children's compliance in pre-school classrooms: a descriptive analysis', *Journal of Applied Behavior Analysis*, Vol. 21, No. 2, pp. 157–67.

Axline, V.M. (1989) *Play Therapy*, Edinburgh: Churchill Livingstone.

Baker, C., Davies, N. and Stallard, T. (1985) 'Prevalence of behaviour problems in primary school children in North Wales', *British Journal of Special Education*, Vol. 12, No. 1, pp. 19–26.

Ballard, K.D. (1991) 'Assessment for early intervention; evaluating child development and learning in context', in D. Mitchell and R.I. Brown (eds) *Early Intervention Studies for Young Children with Special Needs*, London: Chapman and Hall.

Barrett, H. (2000) 'The politics and chemistry of early intervention', *Emotional and Behavioural Difficulties*, Vol. 5, No. 2, pp. 3–9.

Bauer, A.M. and Shea, T.M. (1989) *Teaching Exceptional Students in Your Classroom*, Boston: Allyn and Bacon.

Behar, L. and Stringfield, S. (1974) 'A behavior rating scale for the preschool child', *Developmental Psychology*, Vol. 10, No. 5, pp. 601–10.

Beverly, C.L. and Thomas, S. B. (1999) 'Family assessment and collaboration building: conjoined processes', *International Journal of Disability, Development and Education*, Vol. 46, No. 2, pp. 179–97.

Biehler, R.F. (1981) *Child Development. An Introduction*, Boston: Houghton Mifflin Co.

Borg, G.M. and Falzon, S.M. (1989) 'Primary school teachers' perceptions of pupils' undesirable behaviours', *Educational Studies*, Vol. 15, No. 3, pp. 251–60.

Borg, M.G. and Falzon, S.M. (1990) 'Teachers' perceptions of primary school children's undesirable behaviours. The effects of teaching experience, pupils' age, sex and ability stream', *British Journal of Educational Psychology*, Vol. 60, pp. 220–6.

Bower, E.M. (1982) 'Defining emotional disturbance, public policy and research', *Psychology in the Schools*, Vol. 19, pp. 55–60.

Bowlby, J. (1979) *The Making and Breaking of Affectional Bonds*, London: Tavistock.

Bowman, I. (1990) 'Curriculum support and the continuum of emotional and behavioural difficulties', in P. Evans and V. Varma (eds) *Special Education: Past, Present, and Future*, London: The Falmer Press.

Bronfenbrenner, U. (1979) *The Ecology of Human Development: Experiments by Nature and Design*, Cambridge, MA: Harvard University Press.

Bronson, M. B. (2000) *Self-Regulation in Early Childhood*, New York: The Guilford Press.

Brophy, J.E. (1985) 'Teacher–student interaction', in J. Dusek (ed.) *Teacher Expectancies*, Hillsdale, NJ: Lawrence Erlbaum Associates.

Brophy, J.E. and Good, T.L. (1974) *Teacher–Student Relationships: Causes and Consequences*, New York: Holt, Rinehart and Winston.

Brophy, J.E. and Rohrkemper, M.M. (1981) 'The influence of problem ownership on teachers' perceptions of and strategies for coping with problem students', *Journal of Educational Psychology*, Vol. 73, No. 3, pp. 295–311.

Brown, J.E. (1986) 'The use of paradoxical intention with oppositional behavior in the classroom', *Psychology in the Schools*, Vol. 23, pp. 77–81.

Brown, W.H., Musick, K.K., Conroy, M. and Schaeffer, E.H. (2002) 'A proactive approach to promoting young children's compliance', *Beyond Behavior* (winter issue). Online. Available HTTP: http://www.ccbd.net/documents/bb/promote_child_compliance_winter_02.pdf (accessed 10 May 2004).

Bryer, M. (1988) *Planning for Child Care*, London: British Agencies for Adoption and Fostering.

Burden, R. (1981) 'Systems theory and its relevance to schools', in B. Gillham (ed.) *Problem Behaviour in the Secondary Schools*, London: Croom Helm.

Burden, R. (1992) 'Whole-school approaches to disruption: what part can psychology play?', in K. Wheldall (ed.) *Discipline in Schools. Psychological Perspectives on the Elton Report*, London: Routledge.

Burgess, J.W. and Fordyce, W.K. (1989) 'Effects of preschool environments on nonverbal social behavior: toddlers' interpersonal distances to teachers and classmates change with environmental density, classroom design and parent–child interactions', *Journal of Child Psychology and Psychiatry*, Vol. 30, No. 2, pp. 261–76.

Cameron, J. and Pierce, W.D. (1994) 'Reinforcement, reward and intrinsic motivation: a meta-analysis,' *Review of Educational Research*, Vol. 64, No. 3, pp. 363–423.

Campbell, S.B. (1983) 'Developmental perspectives in child psychopathology', in T.H. Ollendick and M. Hersen (eds) *Handbook of Child Psychopathology*, New York: Plenum Press.

Campbell, S.B. (1989) 'Developmental perspectives', in T.H. Ollendick and M. Hersen (eds) *Handbook of Child Psychopathology* (2nd edn), New York: Plenum Press.

Campbell, S. B. (2002) *Behavior Problems in Preschool Children*, New York: The Guilford Press.

Carpenter, R.L. and Apter, S.J. (1988) 'Research integration of cognitive-emotional interventions for behaviorally disordered children and youth', in M.C. Wang, M.C. Reynolds and H.J. Walberg (eds) *Handbook of Special Education Research and Practice*, Vol. 2, Oxford: Pergamon Press.

Cassidy, S. (1999) 'Under-5s prove to have the write stuff', *Times Educational Supplement* (News and Opinions) 3rd September. ONLINE. Available HTTP: http://www.tes.co.uk/search/search_display.asp?section=Archive&sub_section+News+%.

Chazan, M. (1963) 'Maladjusted pupils: trends in post-war theory and practice', *Educational Research*, Vol. 6, pp. 29–41.

Chazan, M. (1970) 'Maladjusted children', in P. Mittler (ed.) *The Psychological Assessment of Mental and Physical Handicap*, London: Methuen.

Chazan, M. and Laing, A. (1985) 'Teachers' strategies in coping with behaviour difficulties in young children', *Maladjustment and Therapeutic Education*, Vol. 3, No. 3, pp. 11–20.

Chazan, M., Laing, A.F. and Davies, D. (1991) *Helping Five to Eight Year-Olds with Special Educational Needs*, Oxford, UK: Basil Blackwell.

Clarizio, H.F. (1987) 'Differentiating emotionally impaired from socially maladjusted students', *Psychology in the Schools*, Vol. 24, pp. 237–43.

Clarizio, H.F. (1990) 'Assessing severity in behavior disorders: empirically based criteria', *Psychology in the Schools*, Vol. 27, pp. 5–15.

Clarizio, H.F. and McCoy, G.F. (1983) *Behavior Disorders in Children*, New York: Harper and Row.

Clark, A.M. (1986) *Early Experience and the Life Path. The Sixth Vernon-Wall Lecture*, London: British Psychological Society.

Clark, T. (2003) 'Why behaviour training for schools', paper presented at Teacher Training Agency's conference on behaviour management in teaching, Birmingham (March).

Cole, T. (2003) 'The future: new name–same aims', *SEBDA News* (Spring/Summer issue).

Coleman, P. (1998) *Parent, Student and Teacher Collaboration: The Power of Three*, Thousand Oaks, CA: Corwin Press.

Collins, M. (2001) *Circle Time for the Very Young*, Bristol: Lucky Duck Publishing.

Colmar, S. (1988) 'A perspective on behaviour checklists', *Educational Psychology*, Vol. 8, No. 1/2, pp. 117–21.

Conoley, J.C. and Carrington Rotto, P. (1997) 'Ecological interventions with students', in J.L. Swartz and W.E. Martin (eds) *Applied Ecological Psychology for Schools within Communities. Assessment and Intervention*, Mahwah, NJ: Lawrence Erlbaum.

Conroy, M.A., Brown, W.H. and Davis, C. (2001) 'Legal limits. Applying IDEA 1997 disciplinary provisions to preschoolers with challenging behaviours', *Beyond Behaviour* (Fall Issue), pp. 23–6. Online. Available HTTP: www.ccbd.net/documents/bb/ (accessed 12 April 2004).

Cooper, P. (1989) 'Emotional and behavioural difficulties in the real world: a strategy for helping junior school teachers cope with behavioural problems', *Maladjustment and Therapeutic Education*, Vol. 7, No. 3, pp. 178–85.

Cooper, P. (1990) 'Turn on, tune in and co-operate. An interpersonal skills approach to emotional and behavioural problems in schools', *Maladjustment and Therapeutic Education*, Vol. 8, No. 2, pp. 83–95.

Cooper, P. and Upton, G. (1990) 'An ecosystemic approach to emotional and behavioural difficulties in schools', *Educational Psychology*, Vol. 10, No. 4, pp. 301–21.

Cooper, P. and Upton, G. (1992) 'An ecosystemic approach to classroom behaviour problems', in K. Wheldall (ed.) *Discipline in Schools. Psychological Perspectives on the Elton Report*, London: Routledge.

Cooper-Epanchin, B. and Monson, L.B. (1982) 'Affective education', in J.L. Paul and B. Cooper-Epanchin (eds) *Emotional Disturbance in Children*, Columbus: Merrill Publishing.

Cullinan, D. and Epstein, M.H. (1982) 'Administrative definitions of behaviour disorders: status and directions', in F.H. Wood and K.C. Lakin (eds) *Disturbing, Disordered or Disturbed*, Reston, VA: Council for Exceptional Children.

Curtiss, V.S., Mathur, S.R. and Rutherford, R.B., Jr (2002) 'Developing behavioral intervention plans: a step-by-step approach', *Beyond Behavior* (Winter Issue), pp. 28–31. Online. Available HTTP: www.ccbd.net/documents/bb/developing_a_BIP_winter_02.pdf (accessed 12 April 2004).

Dadson, S. and Horner, R.H. (1993) 'Manipulating setting events to decrease problem behaviors: a case study', *TEACHING Exceptional Children*, Vol. 25, No. 3, pp. 53–5.

David, K. (1989) 'The involvement of outside agencies', in T. Charlton and K. David (eds) *Managing Misbehaviour. Strategies for Effective Management of Behaviour in Schools*, Basingstoke: Macmillan Education.

Davie, R. (1986) 'Understanding behaviour problems', *Maladjustment and Therapeutic Education*, Vol. 4, No. 1, pp. 2–11.

Davie, R. (1989) 'Behaviour problems and the teacher', in T. Charlton and K. David (eds) *Managing Misbehaviour. Strategies for Effective Management of Behaviour in Schools*, Basingstoke: Macmillan Education.

Davie, R., Butler, N. and Goldstein, H. (1972) *From Birth to Seven. A Report for the National Child Development Study*, London: Longman and the National Children's Bureau.

Davies, J. and Brember, I. (1991) 'The effects of gender and attendance period on children's adjustment to nursery classes', *British Educational Research Journal*, Vol. 17, No. 1, pp. 73–82.

Davis, P. and Florian, L. with Ainscow, M., Dyson, A., Farrell, P., Hick, P., Humphrey, N., Jenkins, P., Kaplan, I., Palmer, S., Parkinson, G., Polat, F., Reason, E., Byers, R., Dee, L., Kershner, R. and Rouse, M. (2004) *Teaching Strategies and Approaches for Pupils with Special Educational Needs: A Scoping Study*, Research Report 516, London: DfES.

Defalco, K. (1997) 'Educator's commentary', in P. Salovey and D.J. Sluyter (eds) *Emotional Development and Emotional Intelligence. Educational Implications*, New York: Basic Books.

Demers, M. and Gudgeon, C. (2004) 'Abbott and Costello meet the multi-disciplinary team', *The International Child and Youth Care Network*, Issue 60 (January). Online. Available HTTP: www.cyc-net.org/cyc-online/cycol-1203–ellis.html (accessed 25 March 2004).

Denscombe, M. (1985) *Classroom Control. A Sociological Perspective*, London: G. Allen and Unwin.

DES (1955) *Report of the Committee on Maladjusted Children* (The Underwood Report), London: HMSO.

DES (1978) *Special Educational Needs* (The Warnock Report), London: HMSO.

DfE (1994) *The Education of Children with Emotional and Behavioural Difficulties*, Circular 9/94 DH LAC (94) 9.

DfEE (1997) *Excellence for All Children. Meeting Special Educational Needs.* London: DfEE.

DfEE (1998) *Meeting Special Educational Needs. A Programme for Action.* London: DfEE.

DfEE and QCA (2000) *Curriculum Guidance for the Foundation Stage*, London: QCA.

DfES (2001a) *Special Educational Needs Code of Practice*, London: DfES.

DfES (2001b) *Promoting Children's Mental Health within Early Years and School Settings*, London: DfES.

DfES (2002) *Intervening Early. A 'Snapshot' of Approaches Primary Schools Can Use to Help Children Get the Best from School*, Nottingham: DfES.

DfES and DoH (2002) *Guidance on the Use of Restrictive Physical Interventions for Staff Working with Children and Adults who Display Extreme Behaviour in Association with Learning Disability and/or Autistic Spectrum Disorders*, Darlington: DfES.

DfES and QCA (2003) *Foundation Stage Profile Handbook*, London: QCA.

Docking, S.W. (1980) *Control and Discipline in Schools. Perspectives and Approaches*, London: Harper and Row.

DoH, DfEE and HO (2000) *Framework for the Assessment of Children in Need and their Families*, Norwich: The Stationery Office (published with DfEE and Home Office).

Doney, M. (1977) *Interpersonal Judgements in Education*, London: Harper and Row.

Douglas, J. (1989) *Behaviour Problems in Young Children*, London: Tavistock-Routledge.

Dowling, M. (2000) *Young Children's Personal, Social and Emotional Development*, London: Paul Chapman.

Draper, L. and Duffy, B. (2001) 'Working with parents', in G. Pugh (ed.) *Contemporary Issues in the Early Years. Working Collaboratively for Children*, London: Paul Chapman Publishing.

Early Report (2001) 'Preventing and Treating Challenging Behaviour in Young Children', Vol. 21, No. 1, published by the Centre for Early Education and Development, University of Minnesota. Online. Available HTTP: http://education.umn.edu/ceed/publications/earlyreport/spring01.htm (accessed 22 April 2003).

Egeland, B., Kalkoske, M., Gottesman, N. and Erickson, M.F. (1990) 'Preschool behaviour problems: stability and factors accounting for change', *Journal of Child Psychology and Psychiatry*, Vol. 31, No. 6, pp. 890–909.

Eliou, M. (1978) 'Those Whom Reform Forgot', *Comparative Education Review*, Vol. 22, No. 1, pp. 60–70.

Elliot, J. and Place, M. (1998) *Children in Difficulty: A Guide to Understanding and Helping*, London: Routledge.

Ellis, J., Hart, S. and Small-McGinley, J. (2003) 'Belonging. The perspectives of "difficult" students on belonging and inclusion in the classroom', *The International Child and Youth Care Network*, Issue 59 (December). Online. Available HTTP: www.cyc-net.org/cyc-online/cycol-1203-ellis.

html (accessed 25 March 2004).

Epstein, M.H., Cullinan, D. and Sabbatino, D.A. (1977) 'State definitions of behavior disorders', *Journal of Special Education*, Vol. 11, No. 4, pp. 417–25.

Epstein, P.B., Detwiler, C.L. and Reitz, A.L. (1985) 'Describing the clients in programs for behaviour disordered children and youth', *Education and Treatment of Children*, Vol. 8, No. 4, pp. 265–73.

Falconer-Hall, L. and Harlatt, Z. (1989) 'In-service training for support teachers', in T. Charlton and K. David (eds) *Managing Misbehaviour. Strategies for Effective Management of Behaviour in School*, Basingstoke: Macmillan Education.

Fantuzzo, J. and Atkins, M. (1992) 'Applied behavior analysis for educators: teacher centred and classroom based', *Journal of Applied Behavior Analysis*, Vol. 25, pp. 37–42.

Fergusson, D.M., Horwood, L.J. and Lawton, J.M. (1990) 'Vulnerability to childhood problems and family social background', *Journal of Child Psychology and Psychiatry*, Vol. 31, No. 7, pp. 1145–60.

Ferri, E. (1976) *Growing Up in a One-Parent Family: A Long-term Study of Child Development*, London: NFER.

Fishbein, H.D. (1984) *The Psychology of Infancy and Childhood*, Hillsdale, NJ: Lawrence Erlbaum Associates.

Fontana, D. (1985) *Classroom Control*, London: The Psychological Society and Methuen.

Fontana, D. (1988) *Psychology for Teachers*, Leicester: BPS.

Ford, T. and Nikapota, A. (2000) 'Teachers' attitudes towards child mental health services', *Psychiatric Bulletin*, Vol. 24, pp. 457–61. Online. Available HTTP: http://pb.rcpsych.org (accessed 11 May 2004).

Foster-Johnson, Z. and Dunlop, G. (1993) 'Using functional assessment to develop effective, individualized interventions for challenging behaviors', *TEACHING Exceptional Children*, Vol. 25, No. 3, pp. 44–52.

Fox, L. and Dunlop, G. (2002) 'Family-centered practices in positive behaviour support', *Beyond Behavior* (Winter Issue), pp. 24–6. Online. Available HTTP: www.ccbd.net/documents/bb/family_positive_support_winter_02.pdf (accessed 12 April 2004).

Fox, L., Vaughn, B.J., Wyatte, M.L. and Dunlap, G. (2002) ' "We can't expect other people to understand": family perspectives on problem behavior', *Exceptional Children*, Vol. 68, No. 4, pp. 437–50.

Fry, P.S. (1983) 'Process measures of problem and non-problem children's classroom behaviour: the influence of teacher behaviour variables', *British Journal of Educational Psychology*, Vol. 53, pp. 79–88.

Furlong, V.J. (1985) *The Deviant Pupil. Sociological Perspectives*, Milton Keynes: Open University Press.

Galloway, D.M. and Goodwin, C. (1987) *The Education of Disturbing Children. Pupils with Learning and Adjustment Difficulties*, London: Longman.

Galloway, D.M., Ball, T., Blomfield, D. and Seyd, R. (1982) *Schools and Disruptive Pupils*, London: Longman.

Galloway, D. (1995) 'Truancy, delinquency and disruption: differential school influences?', *Education Section Review*, Vol. 19, No. 2, pp. 49–53.

Gandini, L. (1998) 'Educational and caring spaces' in C. Edwards, L. Gandini and G. Forman (eds) *The Hundred Languages of Children. The Reggio Emilia Approach–Advanced Reflections*, Greenwich, CT: Ablex Publishing Corporation.

Garfat, T. (2002) 'The use of everyday events in child and youth care work', *The International Child and Youth Care Network*, Issue 39 (April), CYC-ONLINE. Available HTTP: http://www.cyc-net.org/cyc-online/cycol-0402-garfat.html (accessed 25 March 2004).

Gavrilidou, M., De Mesquita, P.B. and Mason, E.J. (1993) 'Greek teachers' judgements about the nature and severity of classroom problems', *School Psychology International*, Vol. 14, No. 2, pp. 169–80.

Geldard, K. and Geldard, D. (1997) *Counselling Children. A Practical Introduction*, London: Sage Publications.

Gelfand, D.M., Jenson, W.R. and Drew, C.J. (1997) *Understanding Child Behavior Disorders*, Fort Worth, TX: Harcourt Brace College Publishers.

Gibbs, M.S. (1982) 'Identification and classification of child psychopathology: a pragmatic analysis of traditional approaches', in J.R. Lachenmeyer and M.S. Gibbs (eds) *Psychopathology in Childhood*, New York: Gardner Press.

Gimpel, G.A. and Holland, M.L. (2003) *Emotional and Behavioral Problems of Young Children. Effective Interventions in the Preschool and Kindergarten Years*, New York: The Guilford Press.

Golding, J. and Rush, D. (1986) 'Temper tantrums and other behaviour problems', in N.R. Butler and J. Golding (eds) *From Birth to Five. A Study of Health and Behaviour of Britain's 5-Year-Olds*, Oxford: Pergamon Press.

Goleman, D. (1996) *Emotional Intelligence. Why It Can Matter More Than IQ*, London: Bloomsbury.

Goleman, D. (1997) 'Emotional intelligence in context', in P. Salovey and D.J. Sluyter (eds) *Emotional Development and Emotional Intelligence. Educational Implications*, New York: Basic Books.

Good, T.L. and Brophy, S.E. (1991) *Looking in Classrooms*, New York: HarperCollins.

Graham, P., Rutter, M. and George, S. (1973) 'Temperamental characteristics as predictors of behavior disorders in children', *American Journal of Orthopsychiatry*, Vol. 43, Part 3, pp. 328–39.

Graubard, P.S. (1973) 'Children with behavioral disabilities', in L. Dunn (ed.) *Exceptional Children in the Schools*, New York: Holt, Rinehart and Winston.

Hallahan, D.P. and Kauffman, J.M. (1988) *Exceptional Children. Introduction to Special Education*, Englewood Cliffs, NJ: Prentice-Hall International.

Halpern, R. (2000) 'Early childhood intervention for low-income children and families' in J.P. Shonkoff and S.J. Meisels (eds) *Handbook of Early Childhood Intervention*, Cambridge: Cambridge University Press.

Hanline, M. F. (1999) 'Developing a preschool play-based curriculum', *International Journal of Disability, Development and Education*, Vol. 46, No. 3, pp. 289–305.

Harden, A., Thomas, J., Evans, J., Scanlon, M. and Sinclair J. (2003) 'Supporting pupils with emotional and behavioural difficulties (EBD) in mainstream primary schools: a systemic review of recent research on strategy effectiveness (1999 to 2002)', in *Research Evidence in Education Library*. London: EPPI-Centre, Social Science Research Unit, Institute of Education.

Hargreaves, D.H. (1975) *Interpersonal Relations and Education*, London: Routledge and Kegan Paul.

Hargreaves, D.H. (1972) *Interpersonal Relations and Education*, London: Routledge and Kegan Paul.

Hargreaves, D.H., Hester, S.K. and Mellor, F.S. (1975) *Deviance in Classrooms*, London: Routledge and Kegan Paul.

Harper, P. and Gray, M. (1997) 'Maps and meaning in life and healing', in K.N. Dwivedi (ed.) *The Therapeutic Use of Stories*, London and New York: Routledge.

Harre, R. and Lamb, R. (eds) (1986) *The Dictionary of Developmental and Educational Psychology*, Oxford: Blackwell.

Hills, T.W. (1987) *Screening for Entry*, ERIC Digest (ERIC Identifier: ED281607).

HMSO (2003) *Every Child Matters. The Consultation Process and Summary of Questions*, Norwich: The Stationery Office.

Hoghuchi, M. (1983) *The Delinquent. Directions for Social Control*, London: Burnett Books.

Horner, R.H., Sugai, G.A. and Todd, A.W. (2001) ' "Data" need not be a four-letter word: using data to improve schoolwide discipline', *Beyond Behavior* (Fall Issue), pp. 20–2. Online. Available HTTP: ccbd.net/documents/bb/datanotbe4letterword.pdf (accessed 12 April 2004).

Hughes, M., Pinkerton, G. and Plewis, I. (1979) 'Children's difficulties on starting infant school', *Journal of Child Psychology and Psychiatry*, Vol. 20, pp. 187–97.

Iacono, T.A. (1999) 'Language intervention in early childhood', *International Journal of Disability, Development and Education*, Vol. 46, No. 3, pp. 383–420.

Ingram, R.E. and Scott, W.D. (1990) 'Cognitive behavior therapy', in A.S. Bellack, M. Hersen and A.E. Kazdin (eds) *International Handbook of Behavior Modification and Therapy* (2nd edn), New York: Plenum.

Institute for Human Development Arizona (2004) *An Overview of Positive Behavior Support*. Online. Available HTTP: www.nau.edu/ihd/positive/ovrvw.html#WHAT (accessed 23 February 2004).

Jacoby, M. (1999) *Jungian Psychotherapy and Contemporary Infant Research*, London: Routledge.

Jamieson, P., Fisher, K., Gilding, T., Taylor, P.G. and Trevitt, A.D.F. (2000) 'Place and space in the design of new environments', *Higher Education Research and Development*, Vol. 19, No. 2, pp. 221–37.

Jenkins, S., Bax, M. and Hart, H. (1980) 'Behavior problems in pre-school children', *Journal of Child Psychology and Psychiatry*, Vol. 21, pp. 5–15.

Jenkins, S., Owen, C., Bax, R. and Hart, H. (1984) 'Continuities of common behavior problems in pre-school children', *Journal of Child Psychology and Psychiatry*, Vol. 25, No. 1, pp. 75–89.

Jones, K., Lock, M., Webb, M. and Webb, T. (1989) 'Working with parents', in T. Charlton and K. David (eds) *Managing Misbehaviour. Strategies for Effective Management of Behaviour in Schools*, Basingstoke: Macmillan Education.

Kagan, D.M. and Smith, K.E. (1988) 'Beliefs and behaviors of kindergarten teachers', *Educational Research*, Vol. 30, No. 1, pp. 26–35.

Kaplan, P.S. (1988) *The Human Odyssey. Life-Span Development*, St Paul, MN: West Publishing Co.

Käser, R. (1993) 'A change in focus . . . without losing sight of the child', *School Psychology International*, Vol. 14, pp. 5–19.

Kauffman, J.M. (1977) *Characteristics of Children's Behavior Disorders*, Columbus, OH: Merrill.

Kauffman, J.M. (1982) 'An historical perspective on disordered behaviour and an alternative conceptualization of exceptionality', in F.H. Wood and K.C. Lakin (eds) *Disturbing, Disordered or Disturbed*, Reston, VA: The Council for Exceptional Children.

Kauffman, J.M. (1988) 'Lessons in the non-recognition of deviance', in R.B. Rutherford, C.M. Nelson and S.R. Forness (eds) *Bases of Severe Behavioral Disorders of Children and Youth*, Boston: Little, Brown.

Kauffman, J.M. (1989) *Characteristics of Behavior Disorders of Children and Youth*, Columbus, OH: Merrill.

Kavale, K.A., Forness, S.R. and Alper, A.E. (1986) 'Research in behavioral disorders/emotional disturbance: a survey of subject identification criteria', *Behavioral Disorders*, Vol. 11, pp. 159–67.

Kazdin, A.E. (1990) 'Conduct disorders', in A.S. Bellack, M. Hersen and A.E. Kazdin (eds) *International Handbook of Behavior Modification and Therapy* (2nd edn), New York: Plenum.

Kelly, J.F. and Barnard, K.E. (2000) 'Assessment of parent–child interaction: implications for early intervention' in J.P. Shonkoff and S.J. Meisels (eds) *Handbook of Early Childhood Intervention*, Cambridge: Cambridge University Press.

Kerr, M.M. and Nelson, M. (1989) *Strategies for Managing Behavior Problems in the Classroom*, Columbus, OH: Merrill.

Kiley, T.J. and Jensen, R.A. (2003) 'Assessing the climate of an early childhood centre by using key features of organisational culture', *European Early Childhood Education Research Journal*, Vol. 11, No. 2, pp. 77–100.

Killoran, J., Templeman, T.P., Peters, J. and Udell, T. (2001) 'Identifying paraprofessionals' competencies for early intervention and early childhood special education', *TEACHING Exceptional Children*, Vol. 34, No. 1, pp. 68–73.

Kirk, S.A. (1962) *Educating Exceptional Children*, Boston: Houghton Mifflin.

Kohn, M. and Rosman, B.L. (1973) 'A two-factor model of emotional disturbance in the young child: validity and screening efficiency', *Journal of Child Psychology and Psychiatry*, Vol. 14, pp. 31–56.

Konopka, G. (2002) CYC-ONLINE, *Reading for Child and Youth Care Workers*, Issue No. 39. Online. Available HTTP: www.cyc-net.org/cyc-online/cyconline0402.html (accessed 25 March 2004).

Laevers, F., Bogaerts, M. and Moons, J. (1997) *Experiential Education at Work. A Setting with 5 Years Old Manual*, Leuven, Belgium: The Centre for Experiential Education (English publication).

Laevers, F., Vandenbussche, E., Kog, M. and Depondt, L. (no date) *A Process-Oriented Child Monitoring System for Young Children*, Experiential Education Series, No. 2, Leuven, Belgium: The Centre for Experiential Education.

Laing, A.F. (1984) 'The extent and nature of behavioural difficulties in young children', *Links*, Vol. 10, pp. 21–4.

Landreth, G.L. (2002) *Play Therapy. The Art of the Relationship* (2nd edn), New York and Hove: Brunner and Routledge.

Langfeldt, H.P. (1992) 'Teachers' perceptions of problem behaviour: a cross-cultural study between Germany and South Korea', *British Journal of Educational Psychology*, Vol. 62, pp. 217–24.

Lavoritano, J. and Segal, P.B. (1992) 'Evaluating the efficacy of a school counselling program', *Psychology in the Schools*, Vol. 29, pp. 61–70.

Lawrence, D. (1996) *Enhancing Self-Esteem in the Classroom*, London: Paul Chapman Publishing.

Lawrence, J. and Steed, D.M. (1984) 'European voices on disruptive behaviour in schools: definitions, concern and types of behaviour', *British Journal of Educational Studies*, Vol. xxxii, No. 1, pp. 4–17.

Lawrence, J. and Steed, D. (1986) 'Primary school perception of disruptive behaviour', *Educational Studies*, Vol. 12, No. 2, pp. 147–57.

Lawrence, J., Steed, D. and Young, P. (1984) *Disruptive Children – Disruptive Schools?* London: Routledge.

Leach, D. (1977) 'Teachers' perception and problem pupils', *Educational Review*, Vol. 29, pp. 188–203.

Levis, D.J. (1990) 'The experimental and theoretical foundations of behavior modification', in A.S. Bellack, M. Hersen and A.E. Kazdin (eds) *International Handbook of Behavior Modification and Therapy* (2nd edn), New York: Plenum.

Lewis, T.J. (2001) 'Building infrastructure to enhance schoolwide systems of positive behavioural support: essential features of technical assistance', *Beyond Behavior* (Fall issue), pp. 10–12. Online. Available HTTP: www.ccbd.net/documents/bb/buildinginfrastructure.pdf (accessed 24 April 2004).

Lidz, C.S. (1983) 'Emotional disturbance in pre-school children', *TEACHING Exceptional Children*, Vol. 15, No. 3, pp. 164–7.

Linfoot, K., Martin, A.J. and Stephenson, J. (1999) 'Preventing conduct disorders: a study of parental behaviour management and support needs with children aged 3 to 5 years', *International Journal of Disability, Development and Education*, Vol. 46, No. 2, pp. 223–46.

Links, P.S. (1983) 'Community surveys of the prevalence of childhood psychiatric disorders: a review', *Child Development*, Vol. 54, pp. 531–84.

Loo, C.M. (1972) 'The effects of spatial density on the social behaviour of children', *Journal of Applied Social Psychology*, Vol. 4, pp. 372–81.

Lourens, B. (2004) 'Places of emotional safety: creating classrooms where "I can"', Issue 62 (March). *CYC-ONLINE. Reading for Child and Youth Care People*, Online. Available HTTP: www.cyc-net.rg/cyc-online/cycol-0304–childrenfirst.html (accessed 25 March 2004).

Lovell, K. (1958) *Educational Psychology and Children*, London: University of London Press.

Luk, S-L., Leung, P.W-L., Bacon-Shone, J. and Lieh-Mak, F. (1991) 'The structure and prevalence of behavioral problems in Hong Kong preschool children', *Journal of Abnormal Child Psychology*, Vol. 19, No. 2, pp. 219–32.

McAllister Swap, S. (1993) *Developing Home–School Partnerships. From Concepts to Practice*, New York: Teachers College, Columbia University.

McBurnett, K., Hobbs, S.A. and Lahey, B.B. (1989) 'Behavioral treatment', in T.H. Ollendick and M. Hersen (eds) *Handbook of Child Psychopathology* (2nd edn), New York: Plenum Press.

McClellan, D.E. and Katz, L.G. (1993) *Young Children's Social Development: A Checklist*. ERIC Digest (ERIC identifier ED356100).

McCollum, J.A. (2002) 'Influencing the development of young children with disabilities. Current themes in early intervention', *Child and Adolescent Mental Health*, Vol. 7, No. 1, pp. 4–9.

McComas, J.J., Hoch, H. and Mace, F.C. (2000) 'Functional analysis', in E.S. Shapiro and T.R. Kratochwill (eds) *Conducting School-Based Assessment of Child and Adolescent Behavior*, New York: The Guilford Press.

McFarlane, A.H., Bellissimo, A. and Norman, G.R. (1995) 'Family structure, family functioning and adolescent well-being: the transcendent influence of parental style', *Journal of Child Psychology and Psychiatry*, Vol. 36, pp. 847–64.

MacFarlane, J.W., Allen, L. and Honzik, M.P. (1962) *A Developmental Study of the Behavior Problems of Normal Children between Twenty-One Months and Fourteen Years*, Berkeley and Los Angeles, CA: University of California Press.

McGee, R., Sylva, P.A. and Williams, S. (1984) 'Behaviour problems in population of seven-year-old children. Prevalence, stability and types of disorder: a research report', *Journal of Child Psychiatry*, Vol. 25, pp. 251–9.

McGhee, R.L. and Short, R.J. (1991) 'The prevalence of social maladjustment among school-age children', *Psychology in the Schools*, Vol. 28, pp. 285–9.

McGuire, J. and Richman, N. (1986a) 'The prevalence of behaviour problems in three types of pre-school groups', *Journal of Child Psychology and Psychiatry*, Vol. 27, No. 4, pp. 455–72.

McGuire, J. and Richman, N. (1986b) 'Screening for behaviour problems in nurseries: the reliability and validity of the pre-school behaviour checklist', *Journal of Child Psychology and Psychiatry*, Vol. 27, No. 1, pp. 7–32.

McLoughlin, J.A. and Lewis, R.B. (1986) *Assessing Special Students*, Columbus, OH: Merrill.

McNamara, S. (2003) 'Managing Behaviour Creatively', Keynote Speech at the International Conference on Communication, Emotion & Behaviour organised by SEBDA in Leicester, UK (12–14 September).

McNamara, K. and Hollinger, C. (2003) 'Intervention-based assessment: evaluation rates and eligibility findings', *Exceptional Children*, Vol. 69, No. 2, pp. 181–93.

Malone, D.M. (1999) 'Contextual factors informing play-based programme planning', *International Journal of Disability, Development and Education*, Vol. 46, No. 2, pp. 307–24.

Malone, D.M. and Langone, J. (1999) 'Teaching object-related play skills to preschool children with developmental concerns', *International Journal of Disability, Development and Education*, Vol. 46, No. 2, pp. 325–36.

Manning, M., Heron, J. and Marshall, T. (1978) 'Styles of hostility and social interactions at nursery, at school and at home. An extent study of children', in L.A. Hersov and M. Berger (eds) *Aggression and Anti-social Behaviour in Children and Adolescencts*, London: Pergamon.

Martin, M. and Norwich, B. (1991) 'The integration of research findings on classroom management into a programme for use in teacher education', *British Educational Research Journal*, Vol. 17, No. 4, pp. 333–51.

Maughan, B., Mortimore, P., Ouston, J. and Rutter, M. (1980) 'Fifteen thousand hours. A reply to Heath and Clifford', *Oxford Review of Education*, Vol. 6, pp. 289–303.

Mayer, J.D. and Salovey, P. (1997) 'What is emotional intelligence?', in P. Salovey and D.J. Sluyter (eds) *Emotional Development and Emotional Intelligence. Educational Implications*, New York: Basic Books.

Mayhew, J. (1997) *Psychological Change. A Practical Introduction*, London: Macmillan.

Meggitt, C. (1997) *Special Needs Handbook for Health and Social Care*, London: Hodder.

Meisels, S.J. and Atkins-Burnett, S. (2000) 'The elements of early childhood assessment', in J.P. Shonkoff and S.J. Meisels (eds) *Handbook of Early Childhood Intervention*, Cambridge: Cambridge University Press.

Melhuish, E.C. (1993) 'Preschool care and education: lessons from the 20th for the 21st century', *International Journal of Early Years Education*, Vol. 1, No. 2, pp. 19–32.

Mental Health Foundation (no date) *The Big Picture. Promoting Children and Young People's Mental Heath*, London: Mental Health Foundation.

Merrett, F.E. (1981) 'Studies in behaviour modification in British educational settings', *Educational Psychology*, Vol. 1, No. 1, pp. 13–38.

Milan, M.A. (1990) 'Applied behavior analysis', in A.S. Bellack, M. Hersen and A.E. Kazdin (eds) *International Handbook of Behavior Modification and Therapy* (2nd edn), New York: Plenum Press.

Miller, D.T. and Turnbull, W. (1986) 'Expectancies and interpersonal processes', *Annual Review of Psychology*, Vol. 37, pp. 233–56.

Milner, P. and Carolin, B. (1999) 'Introduction', in P. Milner and B. Carolin (eds) *Time to Listen to Children*, London: Routledge.

Molnar, A. and Lindquist, B. (1989) *Changing Behavior in Schools*, San Francisco: Jossey-Bass.

Morgan, D.P. and Jenson, W.R. (1988) *Teaching Behaviorally Disordered Students*, Columbus, OH: Merrill.

Morgan, V. and Dunn, S. (1988) 'Chameleons in the classroom: visible and invisible children in nursery and infant classrooms', *Educational Review*, Vol. 40, No. 1, pp. 3–12.

Morgan, V. and Dunn, S. (1990) 'Management strategies and gender differences in nursery and infant classrooms', *Research in Education*, Vol. 44, pp. 81–91.

Mortimore, P., Davies, J., Varlaam, A. and West, A. with Devine, P. and Mazza, J. (1983) *Behaviour Problems in Schools. An Evaluation of Support Centres*, London: Croom Helm.

Mowder, B.A. and Widerstrom, A.H. (1986) 'Philosophical differences between early childhood education and special education: issues for school psychologists', *Psychology in the Schools*, Vol. 23, pp. 171–4.

Murgatroyd, S. (1985) *Counselling and Helping*, London: BPS.

Musick, J. and Stott, F (2000) 'Paraprofessionals revisited and reconsidered', in J.P. Shonkoff and S.J. Meisels (eds) *Handbook of Early Childhood Intervention*, Cambridge: Cambridge University Press.

Neisworth, J.T. and Bagnato, S.J. (1988) 'Assessment in early childhood special education. A typology of dependent measure', in S.L. Odom and M.B. Karnes (eds) *Early Intervention for Infants and Children with Handicaps. An Empirical Base*, Baltimore, MD: Paul H. Bookes Publishing Co.

Nelson, C.M. and Rutherford, R.B., Jr (1988) 'Behavioral interventions with behaviorally disordered students', in M.C. Wang, M.C. Reynolds and H.J. Walberg (eds) *Handbook of Special Education. Research and Practice*, Vol. 2, Mildly Handicapped Conditions, Oxford: Pergamon Press.

Nikolopoulou, A.K. and Oakland, T. (1990) 'School psychology in Greece', *School Psychology International*, Vol. 11, pp. 147–54.

NPPS (2000) *Age-Appropriate Design Guidelines for Playgrounds*. Online. Available HTTP: http://www.uni.edu/playground/tips/SAFE/ageappr_guidelines.html. (accessed 6 April 2002).

O'Brien, T. (1998) *Promoting Positive Behaviour*, London: David Fulton Publishers.

O'Donnell, J.P. and Cress, J.N. (1975) 'Dimensions of behavior problems among Oglala Sioux adolescents', *Journal of Abnormal Child Psychology*, Vol. 3, pp. 163–9.

O'Hagan, M. and Smith, M. (1993) *Special Issues in Child Care*, London: Baillière Tindall.

Panter, S. (1992) 'Working with parents of mainstream pupils' opportunities and limitations', *Therapeutic Care and Education*, Vol. 1, No. 2, pp. 112–17.

Papatheodorou, T. (1990) 'Teachers' perceptions of children's behaviour problems in nursery classes in Greece', M.Ed. dissertation, University of Wales College of Cardiff.

Papatheodorou, T. (1993) 'Teachers' attitudes towards children's behaviour problems in nursery classes in Greece', *International Journal of Early Years Education*, Vol. 1, No. 3, pp. 35–48.

Papatheodorou, T. (1995) 'Teachers' attitudes towards behaviour problems in nursery classes in Greece and management techniques rmployed', unpublished PhD thesis, University of Wales College of Cardiff.

Papatheodorou, T. (2000) 'Management approaches employed by teachers to deal with children's behaviour problems in nursery classes', *School Psychology International*, Vol. 21, No. 4, pp. 415–40.

Papatheodorou, T. (2002a) *Behaviour Problems in the Early Years* (Module for continuing professional development, University of Ioannina, Greece).

Papatheodorou, T. (2002b) 'How we like our school to be . . . pupils' voices', *European Education Research Journal*, Vol. 1, No. 3, pp. 445–67.

Papatheodorou, T. (2004) *Story Playing for Emotional Literacy and Learning Support* (SPELLS), Project in progress.

Papatheodorou, T. and Gill, J. (2001) 'Imagination and mythic thinking in children's narratives: young children explain the non-logical/rational elements of stories and their experiences', Paper presented at the 11th EECERA Conference, Alkmaar, The Netherlands.

Papatheodorou, T. and Gill, J. (2002) 'Father Christmas: just a story?', *International Journal of Children's Spirituality*, Vol. 7, No. 3, pp. 329–44.

Pascal, C. (2003) 'Effective early learning: an act of practical theory', *European Early Childhood Education Research Journal*, Vol. 11, No. 2, pp. 7–28.

Paul, J.L. (1982a) 'Emotional disturbance in children', in J.L. Paul, and B.C. Epanchin (eds) *Emotional Disturbance in Children*, Columbus, OH: Merril.

Peck, C.A., Killen, C.C. and Baumgart, D. (1989) 'Increasing implementation of special education instruction in mainstream pre-schools: direct and generalized effects of non-directive consultation', *Journal of Applied Behavior Analysis*, Vol. 22, pp. 197–210.

Pellegrini, A.D. (1987) *Applied Child Study: A Developmental Approach*, Hillsdale, NJ: Lawrence Erlbaum Associates.

Peterson, D.R. (1961) 'Behaviour problems of middle childhood', *Journal of Consulting Psychology*, Vol. 25, pp. 205–9.

Phillips, D.D. (1986) 'Reciprocal personal constructs of teachers and pupils in secondary schools, elicited by repertory grid techniques', unpublished Ph.D. thesis, University College of Cardiff.

Porter, L. (2000) *Behaviour in Schools. Theory and Practice for Teachers*, Buckingham: Open University Press.

Porter, L. (2003) *Young Children's Behaviour. Practical Approaches for Caregivers and Teachers*, London: Paul Chapman Publishing.

Powis, P. (2002) 'A process-oriented in-service training model of childcare personnel', *The International Child and Youth Care Network*, Issue 45,

(October). Online. Available HTTP: www.cyc-net.ogr/cyc-online/cycol-1002-powis.html (accessed 12 April 2004).

Presland, S. (1989) 'Behavioural approaches', in T. Charlton and K. David (eds) *Managing Misbehaviour. Strategies for Effective Management of Behaviour in Schools*, Basingstoke: Macmillan Education.

Pretti-Frontczak, K., Kowalski, K. and Douglas Brown, R. (2002) 'Preschool teachers' use of assessments and curricula: a statewide examination', *Exceptional Children*, Vol. 69, No. 1, pp. 109–23.

Prugh, D.G., Engel, M. and Morse, W.S. (1975) 'Emotional disturbance in children', in N. Hobbs (ed.) *Issues in the Classification of Children*, Vol. 1, San Francisco: Jossey-Bass.

Purkey, W.W. and Novak, J.M. (1984) *Inviting School Success: A Self-Concept Approach to Teaching and Learning*, New York: Wadsworth Publishing Co.

Quay, H.C. (1972) 'Patterns of aggression, withdrawal, and immaturity', in H.C. Quay and J.S. Werry (eds) *Psychological Disorders of Childhood*, New York: Wiley.

Quay, H.C. (1986) 'Conduct disorders', in H.C. Quay and J.S. Werry (eds) *Psychological Disorders of Childhood*, New York: John Wiley and Sons.

Quay, H.C., Routh, D.K. and Shapiro, S.K. (1987) 'Psychopathology of childhood: from description to validation', *Annual Review of Psychology*, Vol. 38, pp. 491–532.

Quinn, M.M., Gable, R.A., Rutherford, R.B., Nelson, C.M. and Howell, K.W. (1998) *Addressing Student Problem Behavior. An IEP's Team Introduction to Functional Behavioral Assessment and Behavior Intervention Plans.* Washington, DC: The Center for Effective Collaboration and Practice. Online. Available HTTP: http://cecp.air.org/fba/problembehavior/funcanal.pdf (accessed 26 February 2004).

Rains, P.M., Kitsuse, J.I., Duster, T. and Freidson, E. (1975) 'The labelling approach to deviance', in N. Hobbs (ed.) *Issues in the Classification of Children*, Vol. 1, San Francisco: Jossey-Bass.

Raiser, L. and van Nagel, C. (1980) 'The loophole in Public Law 94–142', *Exceptional Children*, Vol. 46, No. 7, pp. 516–20.

Rajecki, D.W. (1990) *Attitudes*, Sunderland, MA: Sinauer Associates.

Randall, P. (1991) 'Bullies and their victims', *Child Education* (March issue), pp. 50–1.

Redl, F. (1971) 'The concept of the Life Space Interview', in N.J. Long, W.C. Morse and R.G. Newman (eds) *Conflict in the Classroom*, Belmont, CA: Wadsworth.

Reeve, R. and Kauffman, J.M. (1978) 'The behaviour disordered', in N.G. Haring (ed.) *Behavior of Exceptional Children*, Columbus, OH: Merrill.

Reimers, T.M., Wacker, D.P. and Koeppl, G. (1987) 'Acceptability of behavioral interventions: a review of the literature', *School Psychology Review*, Vol. 16, No. 2, pp. 212–27.

Reinert, H.R. and Huang, A. (1987) *Children in Conflict* (3rd edn), Columbus, OH: Merrill.

Rezmierski, V. and Kotre, J. (1974) 'A limited literature review of theory of the psychodynamic model', in W.C. Rhodes. and M.L. Tracy (eds) *A Study of Child Variance*, Vol. 1, *Conceptual Models*, Ann Arbor: The University of Michigan Press.

Rhodes, W.C. (1967) 'The disturbing child: a problem of ecological management', *Exceptional Children*, Vol. 33, pp. 449–55.

Rhodes, W.C. (1974) 'An overview: toward synthesis of models of disturbance', in W.C. Rhodes and M.L. Tracy (eds) *A Study of Child Variance*, Vol. 1, *Conceptual Models*, Ann Arbor: The University of Michigan Press.

Richman, N., Stevenson, J.E. and Graham, P.J. (1975) 'Prevalence of behaviour problems in 3-year-old children. An epidemiological study on a London Borough', *Journal of Child Psychology and Psychiatry*, Vol. 16, pp. 277–87.

Richman, N., Stevenson, J.E. and Graham, P.J. (1982) *Pre-school to School. A Behavioural Study*, London: Academic Press.

RNIB (2000) *A Curriculum for Babies*, Conference title.

Roberts, T. (1983) *Child Management in the Primary School*, London: G. Allen and Unwin.

Rodger, S. and Ziviani, J. (1999) 'Play-based occupational therapy', *International Journal of Disability, Development and Education*, Vol. 46, No. 3, pp. 337–65.

Roff, J.D. and Wirt, R.D. (1984) 'Childhood aggression and social adjustment as antecedents of delinquency', *Journal of Abnormal Child Psychology*, Vol. 12, pp. 111–26.

Rogers, B. (2002) *Classroom Behaviour. A Practical Guide to Effective Teaching, Behaviour Management and Colleague support*, London: Paul Chapman Publishing.

Rogers, C. (1982) *A Social Psychology of Schooling. The Expectancy Process*, London: Routledge and Kegan Paul.

Rolls, E.T. (1999) *The Brain and Emotion*, Oxford: Oxford University Press.

Rubin, K.H. and Clark, L.M. (1983) 'Pre-school teachers' ratings of behavioral problems: observational, sociometric and social-cognitive correlates', *Journal of Abnormal Psychology*, Vol. 11, No. 2, pp. 273–86.

Rubin, R.A. and Balow, B. (1978) 'Prevalence of teacher identified behavior problems: a longitudinal study', *Exceptional Children*, Vol. 45, pp. 102–11.

Russ, D.F. (1974) 'A review of learning and behavior theory as it relates to emotional disturbance in children', in W.C. Rhodes and M.L. Tracy (eds) *A Study of Child Variance*, Vol. 1, *Conceptual Models*, Ann Arbor: The University of Michigan Press.

Rutter, M. (1965) 'Classification and categorization in child psychiatry', *Journal of Child Psychology and Psychiatry*, Vol. 6, pp. 71–8.

Rutter, M. (1977) 'Classification', in M. Rutter and L. Hersov (eds) *Child Psychiatry. Modern Approaches*, Oxford: Blackwell Scientific Publications.

Rutter, M. (1985) 'Family and school influences on behavioural development', *Journal of Child Psychology and Psychiatry*, Vol. 26, No. 3, pp. 349–68.

Rutter, M. (1967) 'A children's behaviour questionnaire for completion by Teachers: preliminary findings, *Journal of Child Psychology and Psychiatry*, Vol. 8, p.11.

Rutter, M. and Garmezy, N. (1983) 'Developmental psychopathology', in P.H. Mussen (ed.) *Handbook of Child Psychology*, New York: John Wiley and Sons.

Rutter, M. and Giller, H. (1983) *Juvenile Delinquency: Trends and Perspectives*, Harmondsworth: Penguin Books.

Rutter, M., Yule, B., Quinton, D., Rowlands, O., Yule, W. and Berger, M. (1974) 'Attainment and adjustment in two geographical areas: III – Some factors accounting for area differences', *British Journal of Psychiatry*, Vol. 125, pp. 520–33.

Rutter, M., Maughan, B., Mortimore, P. and Ouston, J. (1979) *Fifteen Thousand Hours: Secondary Schools and Their Effects on Children*, Milton Keynes: Open Books.

Saarni, C. (1997) 'Emotional competence and self-regulation in childhood', in P. Salovey and D.J. Sluyter (eds) *Emotional Development and Emotional Intelligence. Educational Implications*, New York: Basic Books.

Safran, S.P. and Oswald, K. (2003) 'Positive behaviour supports: can schools reshape disciplinary practices?', *Exceptional Children*, Vol. 69, No. 3, pp. 361–73.

Safran, S.P., Safran, J.S. and Barcikowski, R.S. (1990) 'Predictors of teachers' perceived self-competence in classroom management', *Psychology in the Schools*, Vol. 27, pp. 148–55.

Sagor, M. (1974) 'Biological bases of childhood behavior disorders', in W.C. Rhodes and M.L. Tracy (eds) *A Study of Child Variance*, Vol. 1, *Conceptual Models*, Ann Arbor: The University of Michigan Press.

St James-Roberts, I., Singh, G., Lynn, R. and Jackson, S. (1994) 'Assessing emotional and behavioural problems in reception class school children: factor structure, convergence and prevalence using the PBCL', *British Journal of Educational Psychology*, Vol. 64, pp. 105–18.

Sameroff, A.J. and Fiese, B.H. (2000) 'Transactional regulation: the developmental ecology of early intervention', in J.P. Shonkoff and S.J. Meisels (eds) *Handbook of Early Childhood Intervention*, Cambridge: Cambridge University Press.

Samuels, S.C. (1981) *Disturbed Exceptional Children. An Integrated Approach*, New York: Human Sciences Press.

Sayeed, Z. and Guerin, E. (2000) *Early Years Play. A Happy Medium for Assessment and Intervention*, London: David Fulton Publishers.

Schaffer, R.H. (1998) *Making Decisions about Children* (2nd edn), Oxford: Blackwell.

Schneider, B.H., Kerridge, A. and Katz, J. (1992) 'Teacher acceptance of psychological interventions of varying theoretical orientation', *School Psychology International*, Vol. 13, pp. 291–305.

Schweinhart, L.J., Barnes, H.V. and Weikart, D.P. (1993) *Significant Benefits: The High/Scope Perry Preschool Study through Age 27*, Ypsilanti, MI: High/Scope Press.

Shapiro, E.S. and Kratochwill, T.R. (2000) 'Introduction: conducting a multidimensional behavioural assessment', in E.S. Shapiro and T.R. Kratochwill (eds) *Conducting School-Based Assessment of Child and Adolescent Behavior*, New York: The Guilford Press.

Shea, T. (1978) *Teaching Children and Youth with Behavior Disorders*, Englewood Cliffs, NJ: Prentice-Hall.

Shea, T.M. and Bauer, A.M. (1987) *Teaching Children and Youth with Behavior Disorders*, (2nd edn), Englewood Cliffs, NJ: Prentice-Hall.

Sher, B. (1998) *Self-esteem Games. 300 Fun Activities that Make Children Feel Good about Themselves*, New York: John Wiley & Sons.

Sheridan, M.K., Foley, G.M. and Radlinski, S.H. (1995) *Using the Supportive Play Model: Individualized Intervention in Early Childhood Practice*, New York: Teachers College Press.

Shonkoff, J.P. and Phillips, D.A. (2000) *From Neurons to Neighborhoods*, Washington, DC: National Academy Press.

Sigafoos, J. (1999) 'Editorial. The wages of playing are fun and learning', *International Journal of Disability, Development and Education*, Vol. 46, No. 3, pp. 285–7.

Smith, C.R., Wood, F.H. and Grimes, J. (1988) 'Issues in the identification and placement of behaviorally disordered students', in M.C. Wang, M.C. Reynolds and H.J. Walberg (eds) *Handbook of Special Education. Research and Practice*, Vol. 2, *Mildly Handicapped Conditions*, Oxford: Pergamon Press.

Smith, P.K. and Connolly, K.S. (1980) *The Ecology of Pre-school Behaviour*, Cambridge: Cambridge University Press.

Spence, S.H. (2003) 'Social skills training with children and young people: theory, evidence and practice', *Child and Adolescent Mental Health*, Vol. 8, No. 2, pp. 84–9.

Stewart-Brown, S. (2000) 'Parenting, well-being, health and disease' in A. Buchanan and B. Hudson (eds) *Promoting Children's Well-being*. Oxford: Oxford University Press.

Stott, D.H., Marston, N.C. and Neill, S.J. (1975) *Taxonomy of Behaviour Disturbance*, London: University of London Press.

Sumsion, J.A. (1999) 'A neophyte early childhood teacher's developing relationships with parents: an ecological perspective', *Early Childhood Research & Practice*, Vol. 1, No. 1. Online. Available HTTP: http://ecrp.uiuc.edu/v1n1/sumsion.html (accessed 24 April 2004).

Sutton-Smith, B., Gertmeyer, J. and Meckley, A. (1988) 'Playfighting among pre-school children', *Western Folklore*, July, pp. 161–76.

Sylva, K. and Wiltshire, J. (1993) 'The impact of early learning on children's later development. A review prepared for the RSA inquiry "Start Right"', *European Early Childhood Education Research Journal*, Vol. 1, No. 1, pp. 17–40.

Szasz, T.S. (1972) *The Myth of Mental Illness*, London: Granada Publishing.

Talay-Ongan, A. (2001) 'Early intervention: critical roles of early childhood service providers', *International Journal of Early Years Education*, Vol. 9, No. 3, pp. 221–8.

Tan-Niam, C. (1994) 'Thematic fantasy play: effects on perspective-taking ability of preschool children', *International Journal of Early Years Education*, Vol. 2, No. 1, pp. 5–16.

TES (2000) '*Tests for newborns. Congratulations . . . it's an accountant*' (satirical cartoon by Grizelda) (10 March).

Thomas, A. and Chess, S. (1977) *Temperament and Development*, New York: Brunner-Mazel Publishers.

Thomas, A. and Chess, S. (1984) 'Genesis and evolution of behavioural disorders: from infancy to early adult life', *American Journal of Psychiatry*, Vol. 141, pp. 1–9.

Thomas, D.R., Becker, W.C. and Armstrong, M. (1968) 'Production and elimination of disruptive classroom behavior by systematically varying teachers' behavior', *Journal of Applied Behavior Analysis*, Vol. 1, No. 1, pp. 35–45.

Tharinger, D.J., Laurent, J. and Best, L.R. (1986) 'Classification of children referred for emotional and behavioural problems: a comparison of PL 91-142 SED criteria, DSM-III and the CBCL system', *Journal of School Psychology*, Vol. 24, pp. 111–21.

Tibbetts, T.J., Pike, T.R. and Welch, N. (1986) *Identification and Assessment of the Seriously Emotionally Disturbed Child*, Sacramento: California Department of Education.

Trovato, J., Harris, J., Pryor, C.W. and Wilkinson, S.C. (1992) 'Teachers in regular classrooms: an applied setting for successful behavior programming', *Psychology in the Schools*, Vol. 29, pp. 52–61.

Turnbull, A.P., Turbiville, V. and Turnbull, H.R. (2000) 'Evolution of family-professional partnership', in J.P. Shonkoff and S.J. Meisels (eds) *Handbook of Early Childhood Intervention*, Cambridge: Cambridge University Press.

Tzani, M. (1986) *Themata tis Koinoniologias tis Paedeias* (in Greek) (translation: Topics on the Sociology of Education), Athens: Grigoris Publications.

Ulrich, M.E. and Bauer, A.M. (2003) 'Levels of awareness. A closer look at communication between parents and professionals', *TEACHING Exceptional Children*, Vol. 35, No. 6, pp. 20–3.

Upton, G. (1983) *Educating Children with Behaviour Problems*, Cardiff: Faculty of Education, University College Cardiff.

Upton, G. and Cooper, P. (1990) 'A new perspective on behaviour problems in schools: the ecosystemic approach', *Maladjustment and Therapeutic Education*, Vol. 8, No. 1, pp. 3–18.

Vasta, R., Haith, M.M. and Miller, S.A. (1992) *Child Psychology. The Modern Science*, New York: J. Wiley and Sons.

Veeman, S.A.M. (1987) 'Problems as perceived by new teachers', in N. Hastings and J. Schweiso (eds) *New Directions in Educational Psychology*, London: Falmer Press.

Visser, J. (2002) 'The David Willis lecture 2001. Eternal verities: the strongest links', *Emotional and Behavioural Difficulties*, Vol. 7, No. 2, pp. 68–96.

Walker, H.M., Stieber, S. and O'Neill, R.E. (1990) 'Middle school behavioral profiles of antisocial and at-risk control boys: descriptive and predictive outcomes', *Exceptionality*, Vol. 1, pp. 61–77.

Walker, J.E. and Shea, T.M. (1988) *Behaviour Management. A Practical Approach for Educators*, Columbus, OH: Merrill.

Walker-Hall, J. and Sylva, K. (2001) 'What works with families of children with behaviour problems? Evidence from research', in G. Pugh (ed.) *Contemporary Issues in the Early Years. Working Collaboratively for Children*, London: Paul Chapman Publishing.

Ward, A. (2002) 'Opportunity led work: maximising the possibilities for therapeutic communication in everyday interactions', *Therapeutic Communities*, Vol. 23, No. 2, pp. 111–24.

Watson, S.T. and Steege, M.W. (2003) *Conducting School-Based Functional Behavioral Assessments. A Practitioner's Guide*, New York: The Guilford Press.

Weare, K. (2000) *Promoting Mental, Emotional and Social Health. A Whole School Approach*, London: Routledge.

Weare, K. and Gray, G. (2003) *What Works in Developing Children's Emotional and Social Competence and Wellbeing?* Research Report No. 456. London: DfES.

Webster, J.B. (1989) 'Applying behaviour management principles with limited resources: going it alone', *Maladjustment and Therapeutic Education*, Vol. 7, No. 1, pp. 30–8.

Webster-Stratton, C. (1999) *How to Promote Children's Social and Emotional Competence*, London: Paul Chapman Publishing.

Weiss, S. (2002a) 'How teachers' autobiographies influence their responses to children's behaviours: the psychodynamic concept of transference in classroom life. Part I', *Emotional and Behavioural Difficulties*, Vol. 7, No. 1, pp. 9–18.

Weiss, S. (2002b) 'How teachers' autobiographies influence their responses to children's behaviours: the psychodynamic concept of transference in classroom life. Part II', *Emotional and Behavioural Difficulties*, Vol. 7, No. 2, pp. 109–27.

Weiss, S. (2003) Personal communication (12 September).

Wheatley, M.J. (1992) *Leadership and the New Science*, San Francisco: Berrett-Koehler.

Wheldall, K. and Merrett, F. (1992) 'Effective classroom behaviour management: positive teaching', in K. Wheldall (ed.) *Discipline in Schools. Psychological Perspectives on the Elton Report*, London: Routledge.

Wheldall, K. and Merrett, F. (1988) 'Which classroom behaviours do primary school teachers say they find most troublesome?', *Educational Review*, Vol. 40, No. 1, pp. 13–27.

Wicks-Nelson, R. and Israel, A.C. (1984) *Behavior Disorders of Childhood*, Engelwood Cliffs, NJ: Prentice-Hall.

Wicks-Nelson, R. and Israel, A.C. (1991) *Behavior Disorders of Childhood* (2nd edn), Englewood Cliffs, NJ: Prentice-Hall.

Wilks, F. (1998) *Intelligent Emotion. How to Succeed through Transforming Your Feelings*, London: William Heinemann.

Williams, P. (1991) *The Special Education Handbook. An Introductory Reference*, Milton Keynes: Open University Press.

Wilson, R. (1998) *Special Educational Needs in the Early Years*, London: Routledge.

Wilson, W. (2001) 'The child care worker as a facilitator of family treatment', *The International Child and Youth Care Network*, Online. Available HTTP: www.cyc-net.org/cyc-online/cycol-0501-family.html (accessed 25 March 2004).

Witt, J.C. and Martens, B.K. (1983) 'Assessing the acceptability of behavioural interventions used in classrooms', *Psychology in the Schools*, Vol. 20, pp. 510–17.

Wolery, M. (2000) 'Behavioral and educational approaches to early intervention', in J.P. Shonkoff and S.J. Meisels (eds) *Handbook of Early Childhood Intervention*, Cambridge: Cambridge University Press.

Wood, F. (1982) 'Defining disturbing, disordered and disturbed behavior', in F. Wood and S. Lakin (eds) *Disturbing, Disoriented or Disturbed?*, Reston, VA: Council for Exceptional Children.

Wood, F.H. (1991) 'Cost–benefit considerations in managing the behavior of students with emotional-behavioral disorders', *Preventing School Failure*, Vol. 35, No. 2, pp. 17–23.

Wood, F.H. and Lakin, K.C. (1982) 'Defining emotionally disturbed-behavioral disordered populations for research purposes', in F.H. Wood and K.C. Lakin (eds) *Disturbing, Disordered or Disturbed?* Reston, VA: Council for Exceptional Children.

Woolfe, R. (1981) 'Decision-making', in L. Barton and S. Tomlinson (eds) *Special Education: Policy Practices and Social Issues*, London: Harper and Row.

Zabel, R.H. (1988a) 'Emotional disturbances', *ERIC Digest*, p. 454, Reston, VA: ERIC Clearinghouse on Handicapped and Gifted Children.

Zabel, R.H. (1988b) 'Preparation of teachers for behaviorally disordered students: a review of literature', in M.C. Wang, M.C. Reynolds and H.J. Walberg (eds) *Handbook of Special Education. Research and Practice*, Vol. 2, Oxford: Pergamon Press.

Zabolio McGrath, M. (2002) 'Parallel professionals: working effectively within the teacher–paraprofessional relationship', *Beyond Behavior* (Spring Issue). Online. Available HTTP: http://www.ccbd.net/documents/bb/parallelprofessional29-30.pdf (accessed 11 May 2004).

Index